CHRISTIANITY IN CUMBRIA

The Story of
CHRISTIANITY IN CUMBRIA
a geographical appraisal

by

Henry L. Widdup, M.A.

with a foreword
by the Lord Bishop of Carlisle

Titus Wilson & Son, Ltd.
Kendal

1981

First published 1981

ISBN No. 0 900811 13 7

Printed in England by Titus Wilson, Kendal

To: Professor Emeritus E. G. Bowen
whose help and encouragement have been invaluable.

CONTENTS

ILLUSTRATIONS

Acknowledgements

The author wishes to thank the following who have helped during the preparation of the book: Professor Emeritus E. G. Bowen, M.A., D.Litt., LL.D. (Hon.), D. Univ. (Hon.), F.S.A., formerly Gregynog Professor of Geography and Anthropology in the University of Wales; The Ven. T. R. B. Hodgson, B.D., A.L.C.D., The Archdeacon of West Cumberland; The Rev. Edward T. Scott, formerly the Superintendent Minister, Ambleside Methodist Circuit; Mr. B. Pratt, the Archivist to the Methodist Church, Carlisle District; the late Mr. Herbert G. Swann; The Carlisle Diocesan Registry; The Cumbria Archives Department; The Westmorland Archives Deptartment; The Librarians of Grange-over-Sands, Barrow-in-Furness, Carlisle, Penrith, Whitehaven and Workington; Miss M. H. Bigwood, Department of Botany, University College, Aberystwyth, for specialist cartographical assistance with the numerous maps and diagrams; Mrs. M. Smith who typed the script; Mr. D. G. T. Bloomer who critically read it and Mr. O. Turnbull of Titus Wilson and Son Ltd. who guided it to publication.

H. L. WIDDUP

Grange-over-Sands, October 1980.

Foreword

by
The Right Reverend H. D. Halsey,
The Lord Bishop of Carlisle

The author of this book traces the fascinating story of the spread of Christianity throughout Cumbria and explains how the physical features of the County as well as the changes that were taking place in the country as a whole, influenced and shaped the establishing of churches and chapels both where they were built and how the news of Jesus Christ was carried from one place to another.

The book is well supported by facts and figures and is illustrated with diagrams which will make it valuable for the student, but it is written in such a way that the "man in the pew" who wants to know more about the origins of his own parish and of the Church in Cumbria will also enjoy reading it.

As the Church of today goes forward into the 'eighties through the many revolutionary changes that are taking place the Christian can take heart from this history of the Church which shows how the spreading of the Gospel, the building up of the Church and the formation of lively Christian fellowships may in part be shaped but never confined by the physical facts of the environment.

DAVID CARLIOL

18th September, 1980.

Map 1

MAP OF THE DIOCESE OF CARLISLE IN 1933. (See Appendix)

━━━ Boundary dividing Carlisle Diocese from that of Chester, pre-1856.

CHAPTER 1

The Geographical Background

The term 'Cumbria', throughout the ages, has not always applied to the same area and therefore at the outset some definition is necessary. For the purpose of this book it is taken to be the area of the present day Carlisle Diocese consisting of the former County of Cumberland with the exception of the area to the north of Cross Fell in the South Tyne valley round Alston (in the diocese of Newcastle), the former County of Westmorland and that part of the area north of the sands of Morecambe Bay in the Furness and Cartmel districts, formerly part of the County Palatine of Lancaster. Within the area delineated is the whole of the English Lake District.

It is not intended to give a detailed account of the physical geography of Cumbria for the interested reader will find several excellent books available, but it is necessary to draw attention to certain aspects of it, which have played a significant part in the development of Christian activity.

The dissemination of ideas and beliefs can only come about through human communication by means of the written word (including pictorial illustration) or the spoken word, the latter being by far the more important in the early days before printing was invented, and later before 'Education' became widespread for which incidentally religious organisation was largely responsible. Such communication implies also movement of people and materials whether, in early days, the wanderings of itinerant preachers or the invasion of people with new ideas. Today with the sophisticated methods of travel and the dissemination of ideas and information by means of the mass media of radio, television and recording, human contacts are almost too compulsive.

Those elements of the physical landscape which have affected the movement of people and the location and size of their settlements are relevant and essential for an understanding of the spread, and later consolidation, of Christianity, and this is particularly true when one considers it in terms of distribution and organisation. Nor can one ignore economic and social conditions which have an important part to play in the structure of 'Society', both secular and religious.

Physically (see Map 2) Cumbria has a certain homogeneity. The Irish Sea coast marks its boundary in the south-west in Morecambe Bay, in the west, and in the north-west in the Solway Firth. In the east the Pennines form a fairly continuous wall rising to nearly 3,000 ft. at Cross Fell, but to the north east there is an area of comparative lowland forming the watershed between the Tyne and Eden river systems, the valleys of the South Tyne and the Irthing respectively. This gap between Northumbria in the east and Cumbria in the west of England has played its part throughout the ages; it has always been an important routeway since Roman times when it was also a defensive line in the form of Hadrian's Wall. In the south the valley of the River Lune extends northwards towards Shap Fell, giving access via the Lune gorge near Tebay to the valley of the River Eden at a height of less than 1,000 ft. thus providing a routeway from the Lancashire Plain to the Solway lowlands round Carlisle and the Scottish border. The valley of the River Eden affords a route from the North and West Riding of Yorkshire via Mallerstang and Wensleydale. The routeway between the River Tees and the River Eden at Stainmore should also be noted although it is essentially a highland route to which the frequent wintry conditions on today's A66 road testify.

The largest area of lowland is to the north round Carlisle in the Solway area, stretching inland for more than 15 miles and continuing southwards along the coast with decreasing width almost as far as the district of Furness. If it is accepted that a river basin is an economic unit then the lowest reaches of the Eden and the Solway estuary provide a good example of the problems which arise when such a basin is divided politically. Across this area is the border between England and Scotland, dividing Cumbria from Dumfriesshire and Roxburghshire a purely artificial boundary in the geographical sense, and one which is a recurring theme in the story of Christianity in the area, as indeed in its secular economic story too.

The core of the area is the Lake District mountains with an axis running roughly east-west across its centre from the High Street (2,718 ft.) and Helvellyn (3,118 ft.) range to Scafell (3,212 ft.). There is thus a central 'dome' producing a radial drainage pattern with a

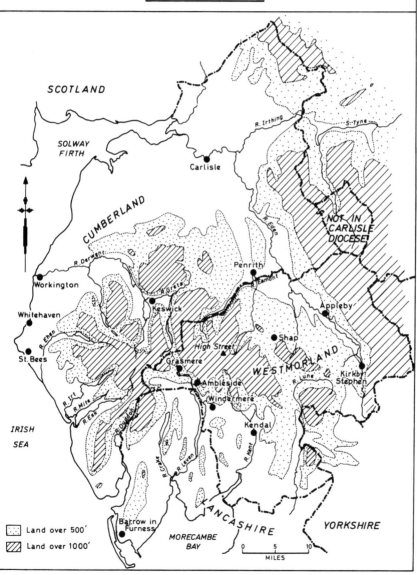

MAJOR RELIEF AND OLD COUNTY BOUNDARIES

Map 2

tendency to north-south. To the north the Eden, already mentioned, and the Derwent, the latter turning westward to enter the sea at Workington; to the south in the Furness, Cartmel and Westmorland areas the Rivers Duddon, Crake, Leven and Kent. These are shorter in length than the mountain rivers but equally important. Flowing westwards, the Irt, Mite and Esk are worthy of mention, reaching the sea at Ravenglass. Thus while the central mountains bred isolation, in many areas the river valleys, most of them deepened by glacial action, allow penetration well inland and give access to the fell slopes – as they did in Viking and medieval days when the uplands began to provide sheep runs. The lower land round this central dome afforded easier routeways (by land and water) and one would expect greater activity on the periphery of the region rather than in its centre. Yet it is important to remember that while the upland nature of Cumbria created problems of accessibility, they were in no way insuperable, as the Romans

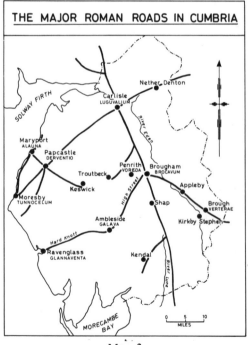

THE MAJOR ROMAN ROADS IN CUMBRIA

Map 3

demonstrated with their road from Brougham over High Street to Ambleside, continuing to Ravenglass via Wrynose and Hardknott Passes (see Map 3). From earliest times movement of people was continuous and considerable in particular areas. The high land did have an effect on size and distribution of population and on its economic viability as it still does. Further it must be appreciated that the visible landscape of today is very different from that of pre-Norman and medieval times. Much of the lowland round the Solway was marshy and much of the rest of Cumbria was forested. It is now thought that even the higher fells were covered with trees and that deforestation took place over many centuries (see Map 4). Marsh and forest militate against settlement and this too affected the growth of Christianity particularly in medieval times.

Map 4

It is not without significance that when the diocese was founded in A.D. 1133, Carlisle should become its Cathedral City. It is a centre on the edge of the region; a centre furthest from the rest of England; a centre bordering on Scotland; a centre which in pre-Norman times was more influenced by Scottish events than English; a centre which had in fact been part of Strathclyde during much of the Dark Ages.

Two other items concerning the relief of the region are pertinent to our story. In lowland areas much deposition has taken place and of two kinds – glacial and alluvial. Morainic deposits from glacial or englacial times are found in many of the peripheral areas of Cumbria and particularly in the Solway region where many drumlins occur (see Map 5). These mounds of unconsolidated material formed excellent dry point sites for settlement in otherwise marshy areas while water was available nearby in permeable rocks.

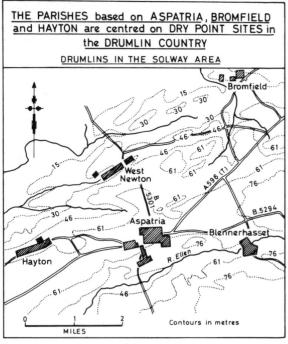

THE PARISHES based on ASPATRIA, BROMFIELD and HAYTON are centred on DRY POINT SITES in the DRUMLIN COUNTRY

DRUMLINS IN THE SOLWAY AREA

Map 5

The lowland areas also consisted of much alluvial material and deep soils resulting from the normal process of weathering thus providing the basis for successful agriculture. The distribution of good agricultural land and the positioning of the great Monastic Houses of the medieval period – Furness, Cartmel, Holm Cultram, Lanercost etc., show marked interrelationship as one would expect for it was on agriculture in the first instance that the wealth of the religious houses was based.

Thus the surface features of relief, drainage, soils, have played a vital role in the religious structure of Cumbria, i.e. the parochial divisions, but that is only part of the story and it is necessary to say something of the geology which too has been important, particularly with the passage of time and ever-increasing technological know-how, culminating in the industrial revolution of the nineteenth century.

The solid geology of Cumbria is the result of a long and complicated evolution which need not detain us in this book, but various aspects of it are of importance. As will be seen from the map (Map 6) the central mainly highland region consists of older palaeozoic rocks of Ordovician age. To the north lie the Skiddaw slates composed mainly of grits, sandstones and clays which have been subjected to upraising and crumpling and pressuring into slates. They extend from Blencathra in the east through Skiddaw to Grassmoor and Ennerdale in the west with other outcrops at Black Combe in the south and the lower part of Ullswater and Haweswater in the east. To the south of the Skiddaw slates also of Ordovician origin lie the Borrowdale volcanic series of rocks comprising thick beds of lava, ash and agglomerates, etc. These extend from Shap Fells in the east, almost to the coast in the south-west with a southern limit through Ambleside and Coniston to Black Combe. Some of the best known uplands and valleys are found in these series – Helvellyn, Scafell, Great Gable, Langdale Pikes, Coniston Old Man of the former and Borrowdale, Langdale, Wasdale, Ennerdale, Grasmere among the latter.

The third element in the older palaeozoics is the Silurian rocks in the southern part of Cumbria stretching right across from east to west and consisting of slate, shale, limestones and flags. In places they reach the northern shores of Morecambe Bay and include the area round Kendal, Windermere and Coniston. Generally speaking they form the lower undulating land approaching sea level in the south. Intruded into these three oldest rock series are igneous rocks of precarboniferous origin. They tend to be on the periphery of the core – the granites of Shap, Eskdale, Wasdale, Muncaster Fell, Skiddaw, the gabbro of Carrock Fell and the granophyre of Ennerdale and Buttermere.

But of greater importance to our survey are the rocks of the newer

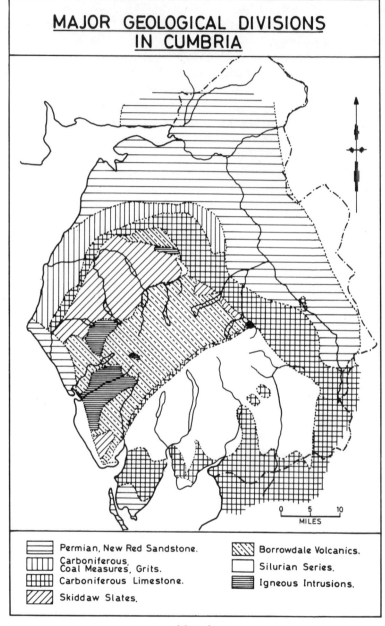

MAJOR GEOLOGICAL DIVISIONS IN CUMBRIA

Legend:
- Permian, New Red Sandstone.
- Carboniferous, Coal Measures, Grits.
- Carboniferous Limestone.
- Skiddaw Slates.
- Borrowdale Volcanics.
- Silurian Series.
- Igneous Intrusions.

MILES 0 5 10

Map 6

palaeozoic era, namely the Carboniferous Limestone and the Coal Measures. These surround the central core in that order. The carboniferous limestone, with inward facing scarps and outfacing dip slopes lie unconformably on the earlier rocks. It is found in the south in the Cartmel and Furness areas, including Whitbarrow, Underbarrow and Grange-over-Sands; south of Kendal in the Carnforth and Arnside areas including Warton Crag; in the Shap area to the east in places like Lowther, Greystoke, part of Inglewood; in the north near Caldbeck and in the west round Whitehaven. The coal measures are beyond the dip slopes of the limestone in West Cumberland in the Whitehaven, Workington and Maryport district (forming the West Cumberland Coalfield) and in other areas of less significance; to the east of Carlisle in the Midgeholme, Hayton and Gellsdale district near Caldbeck and in Westmorland round Stainmore, Barbon, Hartley and Kaber.

Finally comes the Permian New Red Sandstone on the very periphery of Cumbria. These rocks rest unconformably on the Carboniferous limestone and are found principally in West Cumberland and the Whitehaven and St. Bees area giving the characteristic red cliff scenery and in the Vale of Eden, including part of Inglewood forest.

But that is not quite the end of the story for two intrusive elements must be mentioned which at various times in history have affected the population pattern. First in great cavities in the Carboniferous limestone are pockets of iron ore of the haematite variety, non-phosphoric and therefore useful in the Bessemer process of iron smelting and of very high metallic iron content – 54% to 66%. Thus the ore is found in West Cumberland round Whitehaven at places such as Egremont and Cleator, south near Millom and Hodbarrow and in Furness near Lindal and Dalton. Second in cracks and faults in many of the rocks are mineral seams giving a wide variety of products. The Newlands valley near Keswick has proved to be one of the richest districts with copper, lead, and zinc and silver – the now abandoned Goldscope Mine was the best known producer. Other significant areas were Borrowdale for copper and graphite (wad); Coniston for copper; Caldbeck for copper, zinc, iron pyrites, manganese, silver and barytes; Glenridding and Threlkeld for lead. As will be seen later it is the presence of coal and iron ore which has had the greatest impact on the distribution of parishes.

The superficial geology of Cumbria is concerned both with depositional and erosive elements, the former resulting generally in increased fertility of the soil, the latter in less. Again in general terms deposition has taken place in the lower land areas therefore on the periphery, with erosion on the higher lands. Most is of glacial or fluvio glacial origin with peat and salt marshes in places round the coast.

In the upland areas of this central core are the most marked effects of glacial erosion. In the later stages of the ice age valley glaciers radiated from the centre, probably along pre-glacial valleys, but also along fault lines where rock weakness occurred. The result after the final ice retreat was a series of radial valleys such as Langdale, Eskdale, Ennerdale, Wasdale, which were initially isolated and later it is thought mostly tree covered. During the Monastic period after much clearing of woodland they, with their surrounding slopes became the rough grazing land for sheep. In many of the lower reaches of these overdeepened valleys morainic deposits blocked the natural drainage flow and lakes resulted remaining to this day as distinctive features of the area, while some drained away after fluvial erosion, such as the upper part of Borrowdale round Rosthwaite, leaving flat fertile land for farming. As will be seen later, the separate valleys played little part in parish formation until relatively modern times. For instance Ennerdale, Eskdale, Loweswater and Wasdale were in the parish of St. Bees, while Crosthwaite (Keswick) embraced Thirlmere and Borrowdale.

On the periphery it was a very different story. The local ice moving towards the west met the Irish Sea and Scottish ice sheets moving east and south respectively with the result that the coast lands from the Solway to Furness were left with glacial debris in the form of boulder clay – sands and clays particularly in the form of moraines and drumlins. These areas of higher land formed dry point sites above much marsh land and their perviousness enabled them to act as reservoirs for fresh water. These became settlement sites and were therefore very important in parish formation. The main area of drumlin formation in the west is from the Solway coast south to St. Bees and Egremont.

Another area of drumlin formation is found round Kendal in the very south of Cumbria, affecting such villages as Sedgwick, Hincaster and Stainton, and another round Penrith in the Eden valley where there is much flat boulder clay.

Finally in the coastal estuaries there are alluvial elements including peat formation, which when drained as in the Kent estuary provide good agricultural land with a corresponding increase in settlement. To this might be added the broken and hummocky topography of the Silurian rocks in the south, rounded by ice with small fields between providing rough pasture in the less well drained hollows, not without significance for instance in the Staveley, Windermere, Underbarrow area, in which the monasteries had an interest.

Of the physical geographical background it is the relief of the region which has played the most significant part, particularly in the early years in establishing the distributions associated with religious organisation and practice. But the relief is to a considerable extent the result of geological evolution, both solid and superficial, hence the previous description of it. It may be argued that during the nineteenth century the rock distribution superseded the relief in importance, but by then the general religious patterns had been established.

In a consideration therefore of the development of Christianity in the Carlisle diocesan area, geography, as a study of spatial relationships, has an important part to play, and it is suggested that many geographical factors have contributed to the character and ethos of it. It is an area of great individuality, relatively isolated, relatively inward looking which has produced people independent in both mind and spirit.

CHAPTER 2

A.D. 400 to the Norman Period

The Cumbrian story so far as the Dark Ages of Britain is concerned can be divided into three major periods, (a) The Romano-British or Cymric (Celtic) from about 400 to the beginning of the seventh century; (b) The Anglian from the beginning of the seventh century to about 900; and (c) The Scandinavian (Irish Norse) from 900 to the second half of the eleventh century. But they are not clear cut divisions, for the one fused into the other to give continuity of tradition with, therefore, the intermingling of cultures, of language and religious observance. Nor was there a straightforward progression from one to the other as Professor E. G. Bowen points out for example,[1] "With the re-occupation (900-1092) of this area (Cumberland) by the Princes of Strathclyde, the Cumbric language was re-introduced and what Cumbric survived the English and Norse penetrations was in this way considerably strengthened, so that it might even have lingered on there until the beginning of the twelfth century . . . tradition is deeply rooted in the land of Western Britain".

The Romano-British or Celtic period 400 to 600

Information about the development of the Church in post-Roman Britain is difficult to obtain, for much of it is of a circumstantial nature. There are of course no contemporary written records and few actual remains of a religious nature so other factors involved in distributions need to be examined.

Charles Thomas[2] writes "Using such fixed remains as mosaic pavements with Christian symbols, building blocks with Christian graffiti, alleged church sites and, from historical sources the sites of martyrdom and bishops' seats, it is possible to construct a tentative

---

[1] E. G. Bowen, *Saints, Seaways and Settlements* (Cardiff, Univ. of Wales, 1969).
[2] Charles Thomas, *The Early Christian Archaeology of North Britain* (Oxford University, 1971).

map for late Roman Britain that indicates two major zones of Christian activity. One is the extensively Romanized urban-centred region of southern England with a south-east bias. The other runs north-west from the legionary fortress and civil settlement at York to the line of Hadrian's Wall; the Northern Frontier Zone". This northern frontier zone contains the whole of Cumbria.

As will be apparent later, Cumbria was for centuries later to be a backward and remote area, so it is interesting to speculate why Christian activity should be found here so early. During the Roman occupation there must have been constant and considerable movement of people, goods and equipment both military and civilian between the legionary fortresses of York and Chester, and the defensive positions along Hadrian's Wall. In addition, British tribes sent labour gangs from time to time to help in construction and later repairs to the wall. Among such tribes were the Dumnonii from Devonshire and Catuvellauni of the south Midlands and the Durotriges from Dorset. Such movements could only take place if reasonable communication lines were established and the roads constructed across the area (see pp. 4 and 18) bear witness to the way in which any advantage of relief was made use of, or perhaps better, how the disadvantages of relief were overcome. But movement of people and the establishment of communities results in the dissemination of ideas. Does this explain the spread of Christianity in Cumbria, probably through itinerant preachers? And with the departure of the Romans is here seen the continuity of tradition perhaps stronger in more remote and isolated regions?

The evidence of Christian activity can be examined in three ways; first the presence of fixed artefacts, second the distribution of church sites by means of church dedications and third the distribution of Celtic place-names. The second and third are particularly suspect.

Thomas quotes the evidence of three tombstone fragments; one of a possible Christian Greek, Flavius Antigonus Papias at Carlisle, one of Titus at Brougham and one (now lost) with a chi-rho $\chi\rho$ at Maryport. These are of fourth or early fifth century and he deduces from these that some form of Christian group could have existed in the Carlisle area and round the walled civil settlement of Carlisle itself. Further, the recent finding of a milestone at Brougham suggests that there was a 'civitas carvetiorum' in the Eden Valley with either Carlisle as its capital or Brougham or Kirkby Thore if only the upper Eden valley was concerned. Does this in fact imply that Carlisle or its southern hinterland was the centre of religious activity during this period? – and if so did it continue to be after the Romans left? Charles Thomas thinks so and supports the idea that the church in Roman Britain was possibly diocesan and that by the end of the fourth century a bishop was functioning at Carlisle.

In addition, and contemporary with this religious activity, there were many 'wandering' saints or 'perigrini' roaming the lands and seas whose ideas emanated from the Near East, looking for places where they could spend their lives in prayer and meditation, spreading the Christian tradition.[3] They travelled by sea, along routes which included the Cumbrian and Galloway coasts of the Solway region, the Isle of Man, Ireland, Wales, south-west England and Brittany, in other words the periphery of the Celtic Sea, which became a unifying influence in the cultural sense. Thomas[4] for instance considers that the monastic idea (i.e. a permanent enclosed community under an abbot) arrived in the north-west in the early seventh century from the south via the western seaways when the "monastery began to replace the older territorial diocese as the dominant in insular Christianity". Thus the Celtic church fused with the church already established in Roman times.

The distribution of church sites involves evidence of church dedications. Celtic saint dedications are found in churches of pre-Norman foundations, mainly of Norse influence, but it is now thought that the dedications themselves are largely of the eleventh and twelfth centuries representing a period of revival in their cults. The revival of their cults is traditionally associated with their original sphere of influence and as Professor Bowen[5] points out, "the area over which a saint's cult spread is always too distinctive to be the arbitrary creation of the medieval mind".

The largest number of dedications are to St. Kentigern (see Map 7), eight in all, and they would seem to fall into two categories – those four forming an arc across the Solway plain from Irthington in the north-east through Grinsdale and Bromfield to Aspatria in the west, and the four fringing the Skiddaw massif from Crosthwaite (Keswick) round to

---

[3] E. G. Bowen, *Saints, Seaways and Settlements* (Cardiff, Univ. of Wales, 1969).
[4] Charles Thomas, *The Early Christian Archaeology of North Britain* (Oxford University, 1971).
[5] E. G. Bowen, *Settlements of the Celtic Saints in Wales* (Cardiff, 1956).

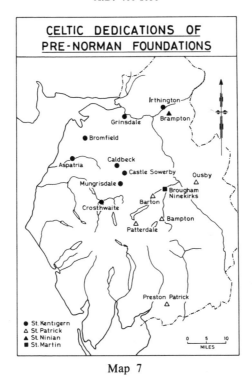

CELTIC DEDICATIONS OF
PRE-NORMAN FOUNDATIONS

Irthington
Grinsdale
Brampton
Bromfield
Caldbeck
Aspatria
Castle Sowerby
Ousby
Mungrisdale
Brougham
Ninekirks
Barton
Crosthwaite
Bampton
Patterdale
Preston Patrick

● St. Kentigern
△ St. Patrick
▲ St. Ninian
■ St. Martin

0 5 10
MILES

Map 7

Mungrisdale, Castle Sowerby and Caldbeck; all are in the northern part of the former Cumberland. Information about St. Kentigern is available[6] the main sources being those of Herbert, Bishop of Glasgow, 1147-1164, and Jocelyn of Furness Abbey who supplied information on request to Bishop Jocelyn of Glasgow 1175-1199. Since Kentigern died in 612[7] there is a gap of over 500 years. The question really arises whether these dedications are in fact indications of his presence as a missionary in Cumbria, as being the positions of his main preaching crosses from which he would speak of the traditions of the Celtic church, or whether they represent the revival of his cult in the twelfth century by Jocelyn of Furness. The latter is now thought to be more likely and in fact there is some doubt whether Kentigern ever moved as

[6] K. H. Jackson, *Studies in the early British church. The sources for the life of St. Kentigern* (Cambridge University, 1958).
[7] *Annalis Cambriae.*

far south as Cumbria since he was first based at Hoddam in Dumfries-shire before moving to Glasgow as bishop. But the northerly position of the sitings would seem to indicate some possible connection with the kingdom of Strathclyde. Speculation can go no further for where does history end and legend begin?

Next in importance to Kentigern comes St. Patrick (d. 461) with five dedications. Four of these are in the area of the middle Eden and the River Eamont, namely Ousby, Barton, Bampton and Patterdale, with the fifth well south in the former Westmorland at Preston Patrick. It is difficult to find an explanation of these sitings, particularly since Thomas suggests that Patrick was a Romanised Briton from a fourth-century Christian family dwelling in the Carlisle area, and possibly consecrated as Bishop at Carlisle and then sent to fill a vacancy in Ireland. But they do come within the pattern of early settlement linked to routeways which cause the dissemination of ideas and strengthen the view that they were a rebound from Ireland when his cult was widespread after the writing of the Book of Armagh, *circa* seventh or eighth century, in which he was portrayed as the 'Apostle of All Ireland', a title he never warranted in his lifetime as a diocesan priest.

Two other saints must be mentioned. St. Ninian has one dedication at Brougham Ninekirks, and St. Martin one at Brampton. Ninian was one of the more important saints of the Celtic church but it was not until three centuries after his death that his name was mentioned by Bede. It is established that his base was at Whithorn in Galloway (Candida Casa), then part of the kingdom of Rheged which also included Carlisle and part of Cumbria. This kingdom was ruled over by the Celtic family of Coel Hen. Ninian's main sphere of influence therefore was south-west Scotland, probably stretching to the Isle of Man and Strathclyde round Glasgow. There is no evidence that he ever set up preaching crosses in Cumbria but it is now suggested by Thomas that he too was a native of Carlisle and was consecrated there before taking up his bishopric at Whithorn. It has been suggested that there is some connection between the Brougham dedication and the existence there of caves suitable for a community of Christians because of its isolation, but this must remain conjectural. The dedication to St. Martin is presumably that of St. Martin of Tours, but there is no evidence of any connection with Cumbria and, as in the case of Patrick he came from north-east Ireland, where his cult flourished. Here again is seen the importance of seaways.

The third possible piece of evidence is concerned with place names. A study of Map 8, shows that British (Celtic) place names are found in the

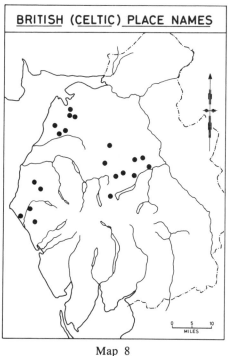

BRITISH (CELTIC) PLACE NAMES

Map 8

north-west of Cumbria along the coastal plain in the Solway and Carlisle areas, and in the area to the north of Ullswater and the middle reaches of the Eden. Place names can be very unreliable as Eckwall[8] points out when he states that Celtic place names were taken over by the Anglo-Saxons and may therefore be of later origin than the period 400-600. It must be remembered that Carlisle, then known as Luel, as later stated by Bede, was the British capital of the area for 250 years after the Romans left. As Cunliffe Shaw writes:[9] "Early in the fifth century the barbarization of the north-west was completed, and the

[8] E. Eckwall, *The Concise Oxford Dictionary of English Place Names* (Oxford University, 1936).
[9] R. Cunliffe Shaw, *Post Roman Carlisle and the Kingdom of the North West* (Preston, 1964).

entire region subject to a British administration who regarded themselves as 'citizens of the Holy Romans', although virtually autonomous. In this part of the country a dynastic complex was developing in the house of Coel for the region of which Carlisle was a major focus, and in the dynasty of Ceretic of Clydesdale and the far south-west of Scotland". The importance of Carlisle at this time strengthens the view that it was the seat of a bishopric. What conclusions can be drawn from the available evidence then about the church established in Cumbria during the British Romano period? The idea that the saintly church dedications indicate the sites of preaching crosses of the saints themselves is no longer thought to be the case, but what is certain is that church site, and the position of fixed artefacts along with place names indicate the existence of people and of settlements. These would be agricultural settlements which were part of freeholders' estates, of which more later. These often had private chapels, looked after by priests, or there were cells such as at Brougham from which preachers went out to the surrounding area. Since settlements were for the most part in woodland clearings there was no strictly defined sphere of influence for the welfare of the inhabitants. The day of the territorially defined parish was not yet.

All the available evidence therefore points to the fact that the Celtic church functioned principally in the lower areas away from the deep valleys and mountains of the Lake District dome, and particularly in the Solway and Carlisle areas and in the middle Eden valley. This indicates a controlling influence of relief and accessibility within the area. No settlement can flourish either materially or spiritually without contact with others so the question of communication lines is important. Before the period under discussion a fairly comprehensive system of roads had been established by the Romans (see Map 3), a system incidentally which has formed the road network up to the present day. There was one main highway from south to north from Lancaster via the Lune and Eden valleys to Carlisle continuing across the Solway into south-west Scotland. At Carlisle it was crossed by an east to west route from Northumbria via the Tyne and Irthing valleys continuing to the coast at Maryport and Moresby via Papcastle. This road ran along the line of Hadrian's Wall. Another came from the east via Stainmore to join the north-south road at Brougham (Brocavum) continuing over High Street to Ambleside (Galava) and then via

Wrynose and Hardknott passes to Ravenglass (Galanhaven). Other less important routes infilled the main framework. Two focal points stand out, Carlisle and Brougham, with perhaps a third at Papcastle. Mention has previously been made too of the importance of seaways as a means of travel, as instanced by Patrick's journey to take over his Irish missionary station, and there is a legend, probably nothing more, that Kentigern established a monastery at St. Asaph in North Wales and St. Asaph was said to be his disciple.

Whether one considers relief as the determining factor in the siting of road routes or not there is naturally a close correlation between the two in Cumbria and both link closely with the human geography of the area. Christian activity is an integral part of this human geography.

The Anglian Period 600 to 900

The beginning of the seventh century saw great changes in Cumbria. Pressure was being exerted from the north and east when groups pillaged and took possession of many of the settlements. That from the north was sporadic and more of nuisance value, for the Picts did not stay, but retreated with their loot; that from the east was enduring. The kingdoms of Bernicia and Deira in north-eastern England had been united under Aethelfrith (593-616) and by 610 he was ready to extend his authority westwards to the coast of the Irish Sea. To the south, by victory at the battle of Chester in 615 he drove a wedge between Wales and the Midlands, and the north-west, while in the north he moved through the Tyne-Irthing gap to Carlisle and the Solway, thus cutting off Scotland from Cumbria. His forces also advanced via Stainmore to the Eden valley. Thus the whole of Cumbria – Cumberland, Westmorland and Lancashire north of the sands, was subjected to Anglianisation both in the secular and the religious sense. For the first time Westmorland (Westmoringaland) and North Lancashire came into the picture, although a few place names such as Cark, Blenket, Roose, Leven and Crake, indicate that the districts of Cartmel and Furness were inhabited in Celtic times. It is more than likely that movement into these last two areas was via the sands of Morecambe Bay since to the north were the mountains and to the east marshes. It was this means of access that had much to do with the development of this area in later centuries. The process of Anglianisation took some time to complete, probably lasting from about 625 to the end of the seventh century. Documentary evidence of this exists in Bede's *Historia Ecclesiastica* written two hundred years later in which he wrote "Aethelfrith conquered more territories from the Britons than any other chieftain or king, either subduing the inhabitants and making them tributary or driving them out and planting the English in their place". He also gives two other pieces of relevant information in that in 685 King Ecgfrith granted to St. Cuthbert, Carlisle (which he named Luel) and 15 miles round it, the area concerned possibly, to provide some revenue from its inhabitants for maintaining religious activities and also that in 678 St. Cuthbert was also presented with land at Cartmel, "With all the Britons therein". This confirms the Anglian interest in the area "north of the sands", in Lancashire. Cunliffe Shaw writes[10] "A series of dynastic alliances with shifting diplomatic sands Anglianised the whole region of the middle and lower Cumbria zone leaving the upper Cumbria of Clydesdale in the hands of the Strathclyde Welsh". We can assume that this lower zone stretched from Dumfries and Galloway in the north to North Lancashire and Westmorland in the south, that is presentday Cumbria plus part of Southern Scotland. This was achieved by the early eighth century, with the first Anglian Bishop of Whithorn, Pechthelin being consecrated in 731. One further comment by Cunliffe Shaw[11] is relevant, "The union of Anglian lordship and Celtic communities with the addition of English settlers produced an individualistic Northumbrian society which formed the heart of civilisation in Carlisle and its region long centuries after the British peoples of Greater Strathclyde, inclusive of Carlisle, had merged with the English to form a unique civilisation in Cumbria which endured until the Norman Conquest and even later times".

From all that has been said, can it be assumed that the Anglians came to occupy areas which were already peopled rather than new ones? Movement into Cumbria would be channelled from the east in four places (1) The Tyne-Irthing gap, (2) Stainmore, (3) Wensleydale and Mallerstang, (4) The Craven (Aire) gap and Lune Valley. As a result Carlisle and the Solway Plain, the Eden valley, and the Morecambe Bay area would be the first to be affected. Confirmation or otherwise of this needs more reliable evidence than is available but some

[10] *Ibid.*
[11] *Ibid.*

help can be given from a study of the distribution of Anglian religious
remains and Anglian place names.

Map 9 shows the distribution of Anglian crosses, fragments of which
are extant today. The most important east-west link was the Tyne-
Irthing routeway in north-east Cumberland where one could perhaps

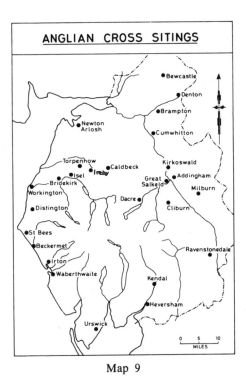

Map 9

expect the greatest concentration. Only four are found in this area, the
most important one at Bewcastle and none in the area round Carlisle.
Further west and south on the lower land and coastal area there are
eleven, the most southerly being at Waberthwaite. Why the gap in the
area round the capital? The routes via Stainmore and Mallerstang focus
on the middle Eden valley and here there are six sites. Here there is some
correlation with Celtic dedications. Only three are found in the Kent,
Cartmel and Furness area in the south. It will be noted that all are
peripheral to the highland area of the central dome and justify the claim

that the Anglians occupied land already peopled, consolidating rather than extending. The Anglian settlers, as the Celts before them, were farmers and therefore the positioning of their settlements was determined by the availability of land for cultivation and the provision of herbage for their animals. A study of Map 4 shows the distribution of woodland in the area at this time. It will be seen that most of the lowland was wooded to some degree and it is now thought that much of the upland was as well. The largest area of dense woodland was just to the south of Carlisle extending some 26 miles from north to south and 10 miles east to west. Smaller areas existed in the lower valley of the Eden and on the Eamont and Lowther rivers in the east and on the Derwent in the west. The largest area to the south of Carlisle was later to be extended and became the Royal Forest of Inglewood. Was this area more difficult to clear? There would certainly be less problem in creating settlements in the other areas, particularly for the Celts who favoured dispersed settlements. The amount of land available for cultivation was to become very important to the church for it depended on it for its income.

Comparison of Maps 9 and 3 show that there was some connection between the Anglian cross sitings and the routeways with focal points round Brougham and Papcastle so it may well be that Anglian chapels were on sites previously occupied by Celtic ones with additions appropriate to an evangelical period. It is known that the Celtic church was dispossessed as early as 664 by the Conference of Whitby when the views of the Roman Church prevailed over that of the Celtic and that during the next 300 years there was considerable development in the organisation of the church although the area was recognised as being one of particular difficulty as stated by Bede in a letter to the Bishop of York 735. "We have heard and it is commonly reported that many townships and villages of our nation are situated among mountains hard of access or in thorny woodland where for many years past no bishop has been seen to confer any of the gifts of the heavenly ministry". The Venerable Bede from the fastness of his monastery was obviously not speaking from first-hand experience! How much of Cumbria would be left if all the woodland and the land over 1,000 ft. in height were removed?

One further source of information needs to be considered in the search for areas occupied by Anglian settlement. Place name evidence is a good indication of previous occupancy, but it is not always easy to

decide, as has previously been mentioned, on the time of inception of
any name, and some of the Anglian names may not have originated
until the eleventh or twelfth centuries. Nevertheless, a general picture
can be obtained even if it is not correct in every detail.

Map 10 indicates such a distribution. It is that of the names of
present parishes in the Carlisle diocese which are Anglian in derivation.

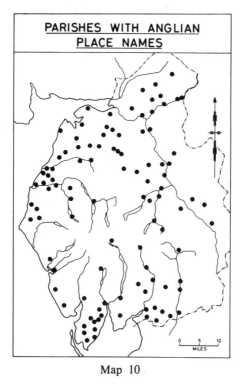

PARISHES WITH ANGLIAN
PLACE NAMES

Map 10

In general their concentration is greatest in the north and north-west on
the lower ground of the Solway Plain, and in the south particularly in
Furness, which oddly is Old Norse, and also in South Westmorland
between the Kent and Lune valleys. They are more scattered in the
Eden valley where in view of the number of Anglian crosses (see Map 9)
one might have expected more. In confirmation of previous comments
the central highland area contains very few, the notable exceptions
being Keswick and Grasmere.

No assertion is made of course that all these settlements are in fact of Anglian origin, nor that those which are, would have had chapels of a permanent nature. Some areas were served by wandering monks with portable altars for the saying of Mass, and no doubt their visits were less than regular. Because of the isolated nature of much of Cumbria it is likely that the authority of the church emanating from the Bishop was not much in evidence, although it was during the Anglian period in England that the offices of Archdeacon and Rural Dean were instituted. But York was a long way away, further than Whithorn had been, and even Glasgow in the days of Ninian and Kentigern.

In view of what has been said previously this region of north-west England probably lagged behind much of the rest of the country churchwise. The Anglians were generally more interested in cultivating the land, since they used the plough, than were the Celts although the latter had instituted strip farming with a share in the waste, which included meadow, moor, cowland, wet pastures and woodland along with any fisheries. This resulted in villages becoming more nucleated, with ownership of land vested in a local freeholding family, the forerunners of the lord of the manor. This was the 'individualistic society', and the 'unique civilisation' spoken of by Cunliffe Shaw (see p. 20). This civilisation survived the Danish invasion of the eighth century in spite of the fact that the organisation of the Anglian church was destroyed. Judging from place name evidence (with qualifications as to its reliability) the Danes entered Cumbria from Yorkshire via Stainmore and/or Mallerstang and proceeded through Kirkby Stephen, Appleby and Penrith down the Eden valley to Carlisle, which was burnt in 876 and left in ruins for close on 200 years. Between Appleby and Penrith there are a number of places ending in BY or THORPE, both Danish suffixes such as Crackenthorpe, Kirkby Thore, Temple Sowerby and Langwathby. Tradition has it that the remains of St. Cuthbert were removed from Lindisfarne on the east coast and carried for seven years through Anglian lands to keep them safe. It is also said that the Bishop of Lindisfarne fled to 'Derwentmouth' (now Workington) en route for Ireland. Prevented by storms from completing the journey he took refuge in Galloway.

Following the custom of the Celts in respect of their freeholders' estates the lords or theyns of the Anglian villages had private chapels owned by them and serviced by a monk or priest who had to take an oath of loyalty to his bishop and was instituted and inducted by him. He acted as the chaplain of the church. He was sustained by the settlement; for instance he was assigned a double portion of the cultivated area compared with that assigned to the villagers. Was this the forerunner of the glebe? In return he had to provide male animals for servicing the herds and flocks of the people. In this way the 'church' became tied to the land – from which in later times great wealth was to flow.[12] Here was the beginning of the 'parson's freehold'. At the same time the lord of the manor and the bishop could claim a proportion of the churches' dues and offerings. At this time too tithes were instituted, usually 1/10th of the value of the fruits of the earth, later to become a compulsory element in the parson's stipend. In this 'secular' situation were all the seeds of the future organisation of the church and the future development of the parochial system. If, as Bede suggests (see p. 22) Cumbria was difficult of access, it may be that it lagged behind the main stream of church development in the rest of England.

One other aspect of the church in Cumbria during the Anglian period is significant. The first of the monastic institutions were founded, one at Dacre (mentioned by Bede as Decore) (see Map 13) and another at Carlisle. How effectively these functioned it is difficult to say.

If it has now been established that Anglian chapels ringed the central dome of the Lake District then it will later be shown how this distribution contributed to the shape and size of the future parishes.

The Scandinavian or Norse – Irish Period to 1050

The Anglian period in north-east England lasted for roughly 300 years up to 900, and it will be recalled that the region had, in the period from the end of the Roman occupation to that date, suffered from tribal incursions from the north, from the struggles for power between Rheged, Strathclyde and Northumbria, yet benefited from the movements of the Celtic Saints as preachers and missionaries and from the establishment of the Roman Church with its organisation, which in fact established the pattern for the future Church of England – far into the future of course.

But by 900, or shortly after, a third element appeared. The Vikings

---

[12] *Cambridge Medieval History*, vol. 6, chap. 16.

from Norway had long roamed the North Sea and the Atlantic in their famous open ships and had pillaged and settled in areas further and further from their homeland. By 700 they were in the Shetland Islands, by 800 in the Orkneys and by 850 in Ireland and the Isle of Man. They also were in Iceland by 870 from which place they were subsequently to cross to Greenland and as we now know, to North America. By 900 there had been considerable fusion between these Norsemen and the Irish and many had accepted Christianity based on the Celtic church traditions. By this time too they had colonised the Isle of Man, which had been on the main routeways between Ireland, South-west Scotland and Wales for many centuries. It was to be expected that they should next turn their attention to the coast of Cumberland and North Lancashire. It is not clear since there are no records, whether they came as pillagers or as peaceful settlers, probably the latter, and it has even been suggested that they came from the Isle of Man as refugees. At any rate the juxtaposition of Anglian and Norse place names (see Maps 10 and 11), suggests that they lived peacefully side by side. They certainly did not come as conquerors in the political sense, for during the first half of the tenth century, as the Anglian influence declined, it was that of Strathclyde which increased and the northern half of Cumbria became a sub-unit of Strathclyde. They are likely to have had some kind of local organisation of government in specific areas of settlement.[13] The southern boundary of Strathclyde was then probably along the River Eamont – later to be the boundary between Cumberland and Westmorland and this situation continued until 1032 when King Canute exchanged Lothian for the northern part of Cumbria, bringing it back again into England. It could well be that the Nordic influence was greater at first in the south in the Cartmel, Furness and Kent areas and it is interesting to note that even today in the twentieth century elements of the Nordic dialect are found in the language of the Flookburgh fishermen. Flookburgh has always been the main fishing centre on the north coast of Morecambe Bay. The writer has talked with a Flookburgh fisherman who joined the navy in 1939 and was sent to Iceland for coastguard duties. He stated that the Icelanders could understand his dialect and that when he went fishing with them he had no difficulty in understanding the terms they used.

[13] Millward & Robinson, *The Lake District* (Eyre & Spottiswoode, London, 1970), p. 148.

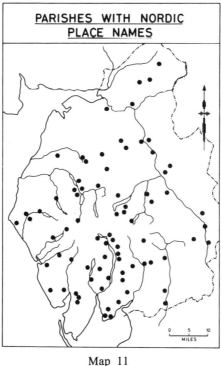

PARISHES WITH NORDIC PLACE NAMES

Map 11

From the religious point of view two types of evidence are available when analysing the Scandinavian element in Cumbria. As in the case of the Anglians, crosses of Nordic origin, but with stray Celtic affinities exist. They are of a wheelback and spiral variety in the main, and with them hogback tombs are also found. They all indicate that the Vikings came as Christians. The Gosforth Cross is the most famous; a Christian monument but retaining pagan symbols of the sagas (see W. Rollinson for details).[14] Map 12 shows a distribution of these Nordic remains. Since the newcomers came by sea it is to be expected that a number are clustered on the coastal plain, and particularly between the River Derwent and the Solway, an area already well peopled; there are three in the area of the Irt estuary at Ravenglass, but remarkably only two in the south, at Urswick and Burton. Another small group (five in

[14] W. Rollinson, *A History of Man in the Lake District* (Dent, 1967).

all) appear in the Eamont district and the upper Eden valley, far from the coast. Mention of this will be made later.

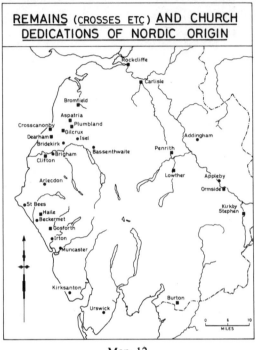

REMAINS (CROSSES ETC) **AND CHURCH DEDICATIONS OF NORDIC ORIGIN**

Map 12

The other type of religious evidence is that of dedication, as with the Anglians, and again it must be stressed not very reliable. The Saints concerned are Celtic in origin as one would expect from a people Christianised by the Celts – Bridget, Michael, Sancton and the mythical Bega. St. Michael is rather the 'odd man out', but the cult of the Archangel spread rapidly along the western seas into western Britain, Ireland and the Isle of Man following the supposed apparition on Mont San Michel in Normandy in the year 710. Their distribution will be found with that of the crosses on Map no. 12. They are, St. Bridget: Beckermet, Bridekirk and Brigham; St. Bega: St. Bees and Bassenthwaite; St. Michael: Addingham, Appleby, Arlecdon, Irton, Isel, Muncaster and Urswick; St. Sancton: Kirksanton. The last is very suspect, being the name of a hamlet between Muncaster and Millom and not a dedication. No further comment is necessary since they conform very much to the pattern of the crosses.

The incidence of Scandinavian place names will give a further clue to the distribution of Viking settlers, with the caveat previously made (see Map 11). This map has been compiled in the same way as that for Anglian place names i.e. twentieth-century parishes in the Carlisle diocese with names of Scandinavian origin, so that valid comparisons can be made. It will be noted that they reach much more towards the central dome than did the Anglian, with greater concentration in the south than in the north of the region. The Windermere-Coniston area is dominant with settlements too well up the river valleys, including the Eden. But in comparison with the Anglians there is little correlation between the place names and the incidence of church dedications and cross remains. The Solway Plain is practically devoid of names – at least so far as present parishes are concerned, whereas the Furness, Cartmel and Windermere areas are devoid of remains. Here is illustrated the problem of trying to find answers without sufficient reliable evidence.

Coming across the sea the Norsemen entered the area via the estuaries and rivers; the Derwent, Irt, Mite and Esk in the west, and the Duddon, Crake, Leven and Kent in the south. The incidence of their names and remains in the Eden and Eamont areas is rather more puzzling. It has been suggested that they made use of the route from Ravenglass via Hardknott and Wrynose to Ambleside or from the south via the Leven and Kent valleys then in both cases via High Street to the Eden Valley. Here again the Roman roads played their part. Thus settlement would first be established on the coastal fringes where already the Anglians lived, and this would involve either dispossessing them or living alongside them. For instance, W. G. Collingwood[15] suggests that the hoard of Northumbrian coins found at Castle Head near Grange-over-Sands (which was then an island in the Kent Estuary), in 1765, may have been hidden when the Anglians took refuge from Viking raids. An interesting but by no means conclusive deduction.

The Vikings were essentially pastoralists, unlike the Anglians who were more interested in tilling the soil, and place name evidence suggests that they moved inland and into the higher areas in search of

[15] W. G. Collingwood, *Northumbrian Crosses of the Pre-Norman Age* (1927).

pasture, clearing woodland and utilising it for the keeping of pigs as such names as Grisedale and Swinside indicate. In this way they were complementary to the Anglians and peaceful co-existence was more likely. Names such as tarn, beck, fell, dale, force, thwaite and booth found in the mountain areas confirm this penetration into the heart of the Lake District dome. The use of 'saeter' in Satterthwaite may even indicate that they practiced transhumance for the 'saeter' or Summer farm still exists in Norway. The penetration gives credence to their settlement in the Upper Eden valley with its necessary highland route means of entry. Recent investigation by biologists at Ellerside Moss near the Leven estuary and also at Blelham tarn just north of Hawkshead has revealed that pollen counts show a decline in oak pollen and a rise in grasses, bracken and heather during the period of the Norse colonisation. This further emphasises the role played by the Norsemen in extending the land suitable for farming and a diminution in the woodland.

It will be recalled that during the Anglian period the churches or chapels of the area were peripheral to the dome. These private churches still remained the basic element of Christian worship some being acquired by the Norse who became landowners and eventually lords of manors. But during the period 900 to 1100 further consolidation of the church took place in spite of a very confused political picture with strife between England and Scotland when Cumberland and the border country was fought over. Grants of land were now being made to Bishops either by the Crown or by private landowners and they began to build churches on their estates. Archdeacons were assigned to definite areas, that of Richmond to the part of Cumbria in the Diocese of York. Such organisation came later however to these areas and it was not really effective until the diocese of Carlisle was created in 1132. In places, Mass was still being said with portable altars by travelling priests.

As settlements developed among the hills chapels began to be built but they were subsidiary to those on the periphery, which eventually were to become the centres of very large parishes, but which at this time began to be burial and baptismal places. It was decreed by King Edgar in 973 that tithes were to be paid to the Baptismal church (Cathedral) except when a private church had a burial place, in which case one third of the tithe could go to the private church.

This was the position when the Normans arrived in England towards the end of the eleventh century. Cumbria was a marginal zone, its· inhabitants a fusion of Celt, Anglian and Irish Norse. Its isolation meant a fairly autonomous church, for the most part determined by freehold farmers and landowners with most churches of a private nature, and situated on the edges of the Lakeland dome. Yet the priests were under the jurisdiction of the Bishop, inducted and instituted by him and with rights already well established in tithes and glebes. The part of Cumbria which was Cumberland was in the Diocese of York, the part which was Westmorland and North Lancashire was also in the Diocese of York and in the archdeaconry of Richmond, sufficiently remote to make supervision difficult.

The three periods of time enumerated at the beginning of this chapter as comprising the period between 400 and 1100 have been dealt with separately, but as stated before the situation was evolving all the time and the coming of the Anglians did not mean the end of Celtic influence. Similarly the Norse did not destroy all the Anglian influence. The three elements in fusion produced a pattern in the human geography of the region which in essence we see today. It is indeed true that here is seen tangible proof of the significance of continuity of tradition, and the stage is set for the next move forward, the formation of the Diocese of Carlisle.

CHAPTER 3

1090-1540 The Norman Period to the Reformation

If the previous chapter has justified the claim that the foundations of the Christian Church in Cumbria were laid during the Pre-Norman period then it is reasonable to claim that its edifice was constructed in the period from about A.D. 1100 to the Reformation, not of course in the doctrinal sense, for Rome was the fountainhead throughout, but in terms of organisation and administration. The diocese, the archdeaconries, the rural deaneries, the parishes – all came to be defined during this period. At this time too there were great changes territorially; in ownership, in political organisation; in land use and all these were bound to have repercussions in the 'Church'. But above all this was a period of constant upheaval in the military sense, for this area was repeatedly ravaged by the incursion of the Scots raiders who looted, burned and pillaged indiscriminately. It is remarkable that any progress could be made in such circumstances when the Bishops had to be politicians, diplomats and soldiers in turn as well as prelates, in order to hold the diocese together. Yet they achieved this, and according to Bishop Moorman[1] the thirteenth century saw the Church in England at the summit of its power. Whether this can be applied to Cumbria is doubtful, but at any rate it survived.

The Normans brought to Cumbria two new dimensions, the one territorial, the other ecclesiastical and these had much to do with the survival and development of the area; the former was in the creation of Baronies, the latter in the introduction of religious orders, which blossomed into the monastic system. Both these created greater stability in both the political and religious sense for they withstood all that the Scottish raiders did to them and in the end achieved strength. This in turn allowed for economic growth, a rise in population with an

---

[1] J. R. H. Moorman, *A History of the Church in England* (Adam & Charles Black, 1967), 2nd ed.

increase in urban dwellers, particularly with the development of market towns.

To what extent did the geography of the area influence the course of events during these 450 years?

At the time of the Norman conquest of England, Cumbria was divided politically into two parts; the area from the Solway Firth in the north to the Eamont in the south including the Vale of Eden and eastwards to the watershed at Stainmore was held by the Scots under Malcolm III, while the southern part, the area round Appleby, the valley of the River Kent and the area north of the Sands was in England and part of Yorkshire. The boundary between England and Scotland stretched right across the Lake District Dome. This explains why Domesday Book contains entries only for the southern part.

After the Battle of Hastings, William I quickly subdued 'Lowland' Britain, most of it within four years of his arrival. But the Highland zone of north-west England proved too much. It was geographically remote from his centre with relatively poor communication lines.

So it was not until 1092 that the northern part came under English sovereignty again, with the arrival in Carlisle of William II "with a large army, and re-established the fortress and built the castle, and drove out Dolfin who had previously ruled the land there, and garrisoned the castle with his men, and afterwards returned to the south and sent thither very many English peasants with wives and stock to dwell there to till the ground".[2] This last point is significant because it implies that previously the area was under-populated and probably not very sympathetic to the English cause. There was to be one more period between 1136 and 1157 when Scotland again controlled that part of Cumbria from the Solway region as far south as the River Esk in the west, but in the meantime William II and particularly his successor Henry I forged ahead with organising this north-west corner of England.

To protect the new border the baronies of Liddell, Levington, Gilsland and Burgh were created, and the barons charged to defend it (not very successfully as time showed). The land of Carlisle, i.e. the inner Solway and lower Eden valley were given to Ranulf de Briquessant (le Meschin) along with the barony of Appleby. Fiefs

[2] *Anglo-Saxon Chronicle.*

(estates) were established in Allerdale 'below' Derwent with the sub-unit the honour of Cockermouth. To the north of the Eamont in the central area and to the east of the Skiddaw massif the barony of Greystoke was carved out, while to the south came the baronies of Appleby in the upper Eden valley and Kendale in the valley of the Kent. The area between Windermere and the Duddon (the Furness area) was granted to Roger Poitou, already a Norman earl. Through marriage Ranulf obtained Kendale and so controlled an area from Lancashire to the Scottish border with his seat at Appleby. When in 1120, Ranulf became Earl of Chester his Cumbria lands reverted to the Crown, and in the reapportioning Henry I kept Carlisle and Inglewood Forest to the south of it which became a 'royal' forest subject to all the restrictions associated with crown forests. There has been much speculation as to how far all these territorial units existed before the arrival of the Normans in some form or other. For instance 'Carlisle and fifteen miles round it was given to St. Cuthbert as far back as 678 (see p. 20) and there is speculation as to whether the Fief of Allerdale 'above' Derwent was not part of the pre-Norman Manor of Hougun, but it will be noted that all these units were in the areas peripheral to the dome of the Lake District, which had already seen Celtic, Anglian and Norse penetration. They were therefore in those areas which had proved to be easier for the invaders; the lower land which was capable of being utilised for farming and therefore for settlement. Further they represent the lines of communication established by the Romans – east-west in the north and north-south in the east – the gateways to the area. Here then is the first use which the Normans made of the geography of the region.

But the territorial story of this period is not quite complete for during the twelfth century the county boundaries were established which were to hold good until 1974. The area north of the sands, the Furness and Cartmel peninsula became part of Lancashire in 1114 because Roger of Poitou owned land in Lancashire and his Furness and Cartmel possession was incorporated with the rest. At the same time the easiest route into this area was from Lancashire "across the sands" there being mountains to the north and swamps to the east in the lower Kent area and it was geographically speaking appropriate that it should go to Lancashire. This is borne out even today when this area has become part of the new county of Cumbria and much discussion has taken place on how to administer it, with the eventual solution of "decentralisation of departments", because there is no one focal point. Towards the end of the twelfth century Cumberland (1178-9) came into being with its capital at Carlisle and comprising the area of Carlisle, Allerdale and Coupland along with the area to the north of the Eamont valley (Barony of Greystoke) and the middle Eden valley. Round the same time came Westmorland (1190) with its capital at Appleby and comprising of the barony of Appleby and that of Kendale. Cumberland was so named after the 'Cymry' the Celtic element, and Westmorland after Westmoringaland, "the district of those living west of the moors". Today all these three areas with small additions have become the one county of Cumbria, thus once again reverting to its Celtic heritage.

It was within this territorial framework that the Diocese of Carlisle came into being. Time had shown that the north-west area could not be effectively controlled from York or Durham or Lindisfarne because of its geographical remoteness, so it was in 1133 by a decree of Pope Innocent II (1130-1143) and by licence of Henry I that the diocese was formed and the canons of Carlisle Priory (see p. 36) elected Adelulf Prior of St. Oswald at Nostell in Yorkshire as first Bishop. It is interesting to note that one of the supporters of Pope Innocent II was St. Bernard of Clairvaux, the founder in 1115 of the Abbey of Clairvaux which became the centre of the Cistercian Order, later to play a most important part in Cumbria during the monastic period. The diocese consisted of the land stretching from the watershed of the Pennines in the east to the river Derwent and the coast in the west, and from the Scottish border in the north to the northern boundary of the Barony of Kendale in the south. This it will be noted was part of what was to become Cumberland and part of the future Westmorland (see Map 1). There would appear to have been little liaison between the ecclesiastical and secular authorities and the southern boundary of the diocese was a better one geographically speaking than that of the county of Cumberland. A river basin makes an economic unit and the higher reaches of the Eden valley in the barony of Appleby would normally be linked with the rest of the valley. This is so in the case of the diocese but not so in that of the County of Cumberland. As the county town of Westmorland, Appleby has never been its main focal point and eventually the County offices were built in Kendal. When the diocese of Carlisle was created the rest of Cumbria – Cumberland south of the Derwent (Coupland), the Barony of Kendale and the area north of the

Sands remained in the diocese of York and the archdeaconry of Richmond. Carlisle began with one archdeaconry and four rural deaneries, those of Carlisle, Allerdale, Cumberland (Penrith area) and Westmorland (Appleby area) (see Map 1). The area covered by the Carlisle diocese was to remain the same until well into the nineteenth century, but the southern part of Cumbria was transferred to the Diocese of Chester in 1541. This will be dealt with later.

The consolidation of Cumbria politically in this period is symbolised by the building of castles — first in some cases as earthworks, later as stone buildings — mainly of course as defences against the Scots. It is interesting to compare what the Normans thought as the main strategic points with the Roman fortifications 1,000 years earlier: near the border Liddell, Irthington (later Naworth), Carlisle and Burgh; along the west coast Cockermouth and Egremont and along the Eden valley Kirkoswald, Brougham, Brough, Appleby and Pendragon. In the south came Kendal(e) and Sizergh. Note these sitings in relation to the main communication lines (see Map 3). But it is not the purpose of this work to discuss military strategy, and in fact these defensive positions seemed to be singularly ineffective in preventing Scottish incursions.

The consolidation of Cumbria from the religious point of view came about in two ways, through the presence of religious houses and through the development of the parish system. Both made their particular contributions and it is difficult to equate the importance of the one with the other, except perhaps to stress the resilience economically of the former in difficult times. The twelfth century has been called the golden age of English Monasticism and certainly during this period many religious houses were set up by the Normans in Cumbria particularly during the first half of the century (see Map 13). The story begins about 1116 when Ranulf (le Meschin) founded a small Benedictine priory at Wetheral which was a cell of the Abbey of St. Mary at York; this of course being some thirty years before the creation of the Carlisle diocese, and Ranulf's brother founded a similar priory in 1125 at St. Bees. The most important house originally was that set up by Henry I in Carlisle itself, the House of the Augustinian Canons Regular which consisted of a group of priests living together and basing their lives on the writings of St. Augustine. It was important because it became the foundation stone of the diocese. The Priory and the Bishopric were one for nearly a hundred years, until 1218, the Canons electing the Bishop and separation came only because the Priory invited the Scots to take over and for ten years wrangling continued. Then followed a number of houses in quick succession, Furness Abbey (1127), a Cistercian House, Calder Abbey (1134), also Cistercian, Holm Cultram Abbey (1150), Cistercian, this last during a period when the Scots were in possession (see p. 56) and it was founded by Prince Henry, son of King David I of Scotland. Conishead Priory (1154), a House of Augustine Canons, was followed by Lanercost (1166) also Augustinian, founded by Robert de Vaux, Lord of Gilsland. Lastly came Cartmel (1188), Augustinian, which incidentally is one of the very few priory buildings in Cumbria to have survived the Reformation unscathed, and the two nunneries of Seaton (1195) and Armathwaite (1200), both Benedictine along with Shap (1199) which was actually founded at Preston Patrick in 1190 and was a Premonstratensian house. The building of these houses took place over a long period of time as resources allowed and as external circumstances permitted, and their influence on this region cannot be over-emphasised. Map 13 shows their distribution, along with other religious organisations of a later date – the Collegiate Churches, the Friars and the Hospitallers, which will be dealt with later. The distribution shows no particular pattern as is to be expected, since they came into being through the gifts of individuals and not through the religious needs of any particular area, with the exception of the Friars, Collegiate Churches and the Hospitallers. They are however all within the areas which the Normans thought fit to share out i.e. the more developed lower lands where revenues were more likely to be obtained. The 'dome' still remained isolated. The exception is perhaps Shap Abbey situated however in the very sheltered valley of the River Lowther cut into the bleak uplands surrounding it.

The importance of the great Abbeys and Priories cannot be over-emphasised since they became the great landlords of the region using their territorial possessions to create material wealth. They were thus in the position to experiment with new methods in agriculture, greatly extending the amount of land in use, particularly by moving into the higher lands and using them for sheep grazing. This was the period when Britain became the chief centre for the woollen trade, and the monks of the north took full advantage of it. The lack of large and beautiful 'wool'-churches which so enhance the landscape of counties

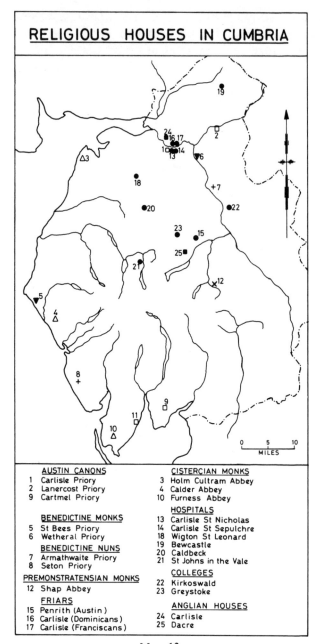

RELIGIOUS HOUSES IN CUMBRIA

AUSTIN CANONS
1 Carlisle Priory
2 Lanercost Priory
9 Cartmel Priory

BENEDICTINE MONKS
5 St Bees Priory
6 Wetheral Priory

BENEDICTINE NUNS
7 Armathwaite Priory
8 Seton Priory

PREMONSTRATENSIAN MONKS
12 Shap Abbey

FRIARS
15 Penrith (Austin)
16 Carlisle (Dominicans)
17 Carlisle (Franciscans)

CISTERCIAN MONKS
3 Holm Cultram Abbey
4 Calder Abbey
10 Furness Abbey

HOSPITALS
13 Carlisle St Nicholas
14 Carlisle St Sepulchre
18 Wigton St Leonard
19 Bewcastle
20 Caldbeck
21 St Johns in the Vale

COLLEGES
22 Kirkoswald
23 Greystoke

ANGLIAN HOUSES
24 Carlisle
25 Dacre

Map 13

like Suffolk with such churches as Lavenham and Long Melford, illustrates just how much the wealth was channelled through the monasteries with the resultant lack of rich merchants to finance church building.

But so far as the Cistercians were concerned the successful channelling took place because of their system of lay brethren who provided a loyal free and devoted labour force in areas difficult of access and scattered yet admirably suited to sheep farming; habitats contrasting with the more nucleated settlements of East Anglia.

The story, therefore, of the monasteries is very relevant to the theme of Christianity in Cumbria and it all occurred between 1100 and 1540. They may have been set up by the Normans as missionary colonies and indeed they serviced large areas of Cumbria in this respect, but their secular significances proved to be equally if not more important. Their importance can perhaps be summed up under four headings. First their effect on religious observances although it is difficult to assess their effect on the development of the church in the diocese of Carlisle and York, and it may be that they went along with the parochial system through their 'secular' members and followed, rather than led, religious observances in the parish churches and chapels accepting the jurisdiction of the Bishops. Through participation they certainly acquired wealth through tithes and were as persistent as anyone else in the system of appropriations (see p. 59) which helped to fill their coffers.

Secondly, as has already been mentioned they became very large landowners, consolidating their holdings in the lowlands by later acquisitions in the higher parts of the Lake District – in the central dome area largely undeveloped until this period. Thirdly, land ownership resulted in their having great influence on land use and while they made use of the feudal system of land tenure they varied it to suit their needs and brought into cultivation much land previously thought to be of little value. Fourthly, they became merchants and traders doing much to foster both internal and external trade, and so along with secular landowners and merchants set the seal on the economic set-up in the British isles which has lasted until today.

Their influence was not confined to the actual localities of their abbeys for the Cistercians were controlled directly from Citeaux, the Mother Abbey and in fact all abbots had to attend the Annual Chapter there and deliberate not only on religious matters, but also on economic ones which affected all Cistercian houses in Western Europe as far as the Middle East. Thus already was established a supranational body of great economic importance acting on behalf of the furtherance of the Christian faith. It was in fact a Common Market in which the woollen trade was predominant, and goes far to explain why the wool trade of Flanders was so well organised and successful.

But these are generalisations and it would be as well to be more precise by example. Since the story of the church tends to concentrate on the northern part of Cumbria the examples of monastic influence can perhaps best come from the southern part i.e. that area north of the Sands of Morecambe Bay until recently in Lancashire i.e. the Furness and Cartmel area. In this area there were three religious houses – Furness Abbey (Cistercian), Conishead Priory (Augustinian) and Cartmel Priory (Augustinian). Of these Furness became the most important. It was founded in 1127 in a rather isolated deep valley originally called Bekangs-Gill about half a mile west of Dalton on the road to what is now Barrow-in-Furness. West[3] in his "Antiquities of Furness", describes it as "opening to the south with an agreeable aspect to the noon-day sun: It is well watered with a rivulet of fine water collected from the adjacent spring and has many convenient places for mills and fish ponds. The situation is gloomy and romantic . . . . The situation of this abbey so favourable to a contemplative life, justifies the choice of its first settlers". What West perhaps failed to appreciate was that Furness was attractive to the Cistercians because of its suitability for sheep farming which was far more important to them than a site fit for 'contemplation'.

But what of the Abbey as landowners? Here is a translation of the foundation charter –[4]

> In the name of the Blessed Trinity, and in honour of St. Mary of Furness, I Stephen, earl of Bologne and Moreton, consulting God, and providing for the safety of my own soul, the soul of my wife the countess Matilda, the soul of my lord and uncle Henry King of England and Duke of Normandy, and for the souls of all the faithful, living as well as dead, in the year of our Lord 1127 of the Roman indication the 5th and 18th of the epact: Considering every day the uncertainty of life that the roses and flowers of kings, emperors and dukes and the crowns and palms of all the great, wither and decay; and that all things, with an uninterrupted course tend to dissolution and death.

[3] Thomas West, *The Antiquities of Furness*, Ulverston (1813), (London, 1774).
[4] *Ibid.*

I therefore return, give and grant to God and St. Mary of Furness, all Furness and Walney with the privilege of hunting; with Dalton, and all my lordship in Furness with the men and everything thereto belonging, that is, in woods and in open grounds in land and in water and Ulverston, and Roger Braithwaite, with all that belongs to him and my fisheries in Lancaster and Little Guoring (Cuorenum Parvum) with all the land thereof; with sac and soc, tol and team, infangenetheof, and everything within Furness, except the lands of Michael le Fleming; with this view, and upon this condition. That in Furness an order of regular monks be by divine permission established; which gift and offering I by supreme authority appoint to be forever observed; and that it may remain firm and inviolate forever I subscribe this charter with my hand, and confirm it with the sign of the Holy Cross.

Signed by
  Henry, King of England and Duke of Normandy
  Thurston, Archbishop of York

  Audin } Bishops
  Boces }

                                    Robert, Keeper of the Seal
                                    Robert, Earle of Gloster

Sac – power of imposing fines upon tenants and vassals within the lordship.
Soc – power and authority of administering justice.
Tol – a duty paid for buying and selling.
Team – A Royalty granted for trying bondmen and villeins, with a sovereign power over their villein tenants, their wives, children and goods to dispose of them at pleasure.
Infangenetheof – the power of judging of theft committed within the liberty of Furness.

Thus at the outset Furness Abbey acquired a very large tract of land with great variety of vegetation resulting from the variety of relief of the holdings, rising from sea level in the south to 2,635 ft. in the north at Coniston Old Man, of variety too of geological formations – of later economic significance. On the west it was bounded by the River Duddon and its estuary, in the north by Wrynose Pass, the River Brathay through Little Langdale to Elterwater and Windermere at Waterhead. Its easterly limit was Windermere and the Leven river and estuary, and Morecambe Bay was to the south (see Map 14). So the Abbey became a powerful landowner from its inception with considerable influence, both spiritually and temporally in an ever-increasing area throughout its life-time. It was not uninterruptedly successful, for Furness suffered from the marauding Scots like the rest

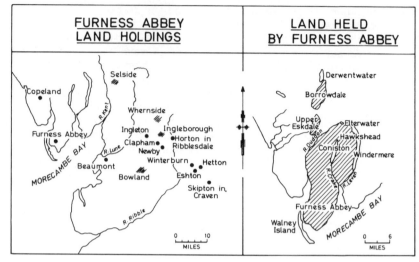

Map 14

of the area, but the overall picture is one of increasing power with successive monarchs confirming its privileges and status. By 1250 the Abbey's influence had stretched far beyond Furness with daughter houses at Calder (1135) and Swinehead (1134) in England, Rusken (1138) in the Isle of Man, and Fermoy (1170), Holy Cross (1180), Corecumruadh (1197), Wotherney (1198) and Inislaunaght (1240) in Ireland. In fact Ireland became the granary for the abbey in spite of the fact that some 2,000 acres in Furness were under wheat and other crops by 1200.

The following summary indicates just how widespread were the interests of Furness Abbey –

There were land holdings at:

(1) Skipton-in-Craven (1138), Hetton and Eshton;
(2) Horton-in-Ribblesdale (1338);
(3) Pastures on slopes of Whernside and Ingleborough (for which the Abbot paid £600 to Alicia of Staveley);
(4) Grants at Clapham, and Newby in West Yorkshire;
(5) Beaumont near Lancaster and Stalmine in Amounderness (Bowland);
(6) Ingleton – 1,000 acres (1316) Selside and Birkwith – 5,000 acres;
(7) Meath in Ireland;
(8) Horvum and Foss in Copeland;

(9) Most of Borrowdale in Cumberland, with extensive rights and free transit through the barony of Allerdale and Copeland granted by Alicia de Rumeli (the area round Stonethwaite and Langstrathdale belonged to Fountains Abbey).

The distribution of these land holdings is shown in Map 14.

The spiritual possessions were the churches of
(1) Dalton and Urswick;
(2) Ulverston and Pennington (at times in dispute with Conishead);
(3) Kirkby Ireleth;
(4) Millom;
(5) Kirk Michael and Kirk Maughold in the Isle of Man.

Other temporal rights and possessions
(1) 3 smithies and 5 watermills in High Furness;
(2) Fishing rights in the River Lune and Morecambe Bay;
(3) The 'Piel' tower of Foudrey (Piel Island);
(4) Digging of turf (peat) and drying of salt on shores of Morecambe Bay;
(5) Fishing on Coniston Water and Windermere.

All this illustrates the fact that while the intention of the Normans in setting up the religious houses was to give opportunity for Christian missions, the result was that they became a vital element in the economic life of the region – perhaps it would be fair to say the overriding element. At the same time their possessions gave them the stability of regular incomes – both cash and kind and status through the privileges accorded them. For instance the cash income of Furness Abbey in 1292 was £40 14s. 8d. as a result of rentals, proceeds from livestock, pleas and mines. In 1535 just before the Dissolution, Parliament ordered a survey of the income of religious houses and that pertaining to Furness gave the following information (given in summary form only):

A survey taken in pursuance of an Act of Parliament, 26 Hen. VIII of the Abbey of Furness in the Archdeaconry of Richmond, and Rural Deanery of Furness and Cartmel, in the county of Lancashire.

	£	s.	d.
Site of Abbey with orchards, mills, etc.	2	0	0
Rent of divers granges, fields, meadows, fisheries within the manor	102	15	8
Rent of Tenement of South End	10	9	0
Rents of Hamlet of Biggar	15	12	0
Rents of Hamlet of Northside	10	14	8
Rent of Tenement of North End	7	0	4
Rent of Hamlet of Cockayne	5	16	8
Rent of Hamlet of Barrayhead	11	0	0

	£	s	d
Rent of Hamlet of Salthous	5	1	4
Rent of Ruse House	1	7	0
Rent of Hamlet of Ruse Cottage	11	1	4
Rent of Rammyssyde	25	5	$11\frac{1}{2}$
Rent of Hawcott and Newbarys	25	13	11
Rent of Marsh Grange	5	6	8
Rent of Hamlet of Hyerlyth	9	7	8
Rent of Yerlyth park etc.	3	12	8
Rent of Vill of Lyndale	12	12	1
Rent of tenement of Aliskayles	4	0	0
Rent of Hamlet of Newton	11	13	10
Rent of Hamlet of Stanke	13	7	8
Rent of Yerlifsydecote		13	4
Rent within Vill of Dalton	34	19	6
Rent within tenement of Bolton	2	7	6
Angerton Moss rents	3	2	4
Ulverston rents	4	2	6
Rent of hamlet of Skathewayt	10	2	4
Rent of Granges in Furness Fells	102	14	$2\frac{1}{2}$
Rent in Hawkshead	2	0	0
Rents of Furness Fell village	44	15	$6\frac{1}{2}$
Rents of villages over Sands	35	1	$2\frac{1}{2}$
Rents of free tenants in several vills.	13	2	4
Rent of Stalmyn Grange	8	6	9
Rent of Winterburn etc.	50	12	6
Rents in Lonsdall	110	18	2
Rents in York	2	0	0
Rents in Ireland	10	0	0
Rents in Borrowdale	32	16	8
Total of temporal rents	£761	13	4

Ecclesiastical Rents in Lancashire

	£	s	d
Tithes of the Rectory of Dalton	39	19	4
Tithes of the Rectory of Urswick	21	0	0
Tithes of the Chapel of Hawkshead	87	10	0

Ecclesiastical rents in Cumberland

	£	s	d
Tithes of the Rectory of Myllom	28	13	4

Ecclesiastical Rents in Man

	£	s	d
Tithes of divers churches	6	13	4

Ecclesiastical Rents in Lancashire

	£	s	d
Priory of Conishead	6	0	0
Total of Ecclesiastical rents	£189	16	0
Sum total of all rents	£951	9	4

In the year 1535 this grand total represented considerable wealth. Much of it was provided in kind and a list of the various commodities gives a good indication of the types of agriculture practised in the area. The following items are named in the above survey: Barley, Oats, Wheat, Cattle, Sheep, Lambs, Wool, Butter, Cheese, Sterks (cattle), Hoggasters (year-old sheep), Hens, Geese, Capons, Salt, Peats. In addition there were Fisheries, Mills and Tanneries.

Of the cereals, oats was by far the most important, followed by wheat, with barley as a poor third (372, 105, 64 quarters respectively). With such large amounts of foodstuffs storage was an obvious problem. This was solved by the building of granges at strategic points, a name which has become part of our vocabulary of place names. Usually these granges were within a day's journey from the centre or from each other. Thus the granges of Beaumont (Lancaster) and Winterburn in Yorkshire were on the route from Furness Abbey via the Sands, to York where the Abbey had property, each a day's journey apart presumably on horseback. By the year 1292 the Abbey possessed eleven granges in the Furness area itself and in 1535 twenty-seven are listed in the survey in the same area, including those at Bouth, Nibthwaite, Oxenpark, Haverthwaite, Graythwaite, Sawrey and Elterwater. There were granges too at Stalmine in Amounderness and at Hawkshead. The rights and privileges granted by successive monarchs and popes must also have been of considerable importance, since for instance the Abbot paid Henry III 4,000 marks for confirmation of such privileges. It must be remembered that the monasteries flourished during the feudal period, when the advantages of land ownership were considerable and patronage rife. For example Henry I confirmed Stephen's grant; thus the Abbot "Claimed free chace through all Furness, and wrecks of sea on the coast of Furness, except in Aldingham . . . he had a free market and fair in Dalton, with a court of criminal jurisdiction; he issued summonses and attachments by his own bailiff in Furness, and granted executions by his bailiff and the kings coroner; he had the return of all writs; and the sheriff, with his officers were prohibited from entering his territories under any pretext of office whatever. His lands and tenants were excempted from all regal exactions of talliage, toll, passage, portage and vectigal; and no man was to presume to disturb or molest, the abbot or any of his tenants, on pain of forfeiting ten pounds to the king".[5]

[5] Thomas West, *The Antiquities of Furness* (Ulverston, 1813).

Pope Eugenius III specifically confirmed his protection for all the possessions of "my beloved son John Abbot of St. Mary's in Furness and to his brethren present and to come", and stated "As to the lands which are cultivated by yourselves, the tithes of them".

The same kind of story continued right up to the Dissolution. But to return to the economics of Furness. The agriculture practiced was mixed and well balanced since it had to be self-sufficient. Thus cereal growing, dairy farming and sheep grazing were all important, but it was the sheep grazing which became commercially most significant. With the possession of High Furness (i.e. the Coniston area), and of much of Borrowdale, the opportunity arose for using higher land outside the enclosed feudal fields and above the tree line for sheep runs, and wool became a marketable commodity with exports on a considerable scale. Piel Castle was built by the Abbot of Furness in 1327, replacing an earlier fortress built of timber during Stephen's reign (1135-54) which was one of the conditions which went with his original grant of land, "that the brethren should make, sustain, repair and guard a fort in defence of these parts". And also no doubt to safeguard the Irish routes. But in the 1423 Rolls of Parliament there was a petition by the merchants of the Calais Staple complaining that Abbot Robert had been smuggling wool out of the kingdom without paying duty and that the monks found the "peil of Foudrey" (Piel Island) a convenient place for the shipping of goods to Ernemouth in Zealand. Since the complaint was from the merchants of the Calais Staple, the 'goods' complained of were no doubt wool. The monks also possessed a building in Beverley which would act as a collecting and distribution point for exporting wool through the Humber.

Another very important right was that of 'mining'. This was first granted in 1270 by Robert Layburn – "all right of getting mine within the abbot's jurisdiction" (viz. iron and copper ore), thus all royalties and profits for mining accrued to the abbey. In about 1510 there were three iron forges in the manor of Hawkshead for which the Abbot received £20 per annum in rent.

At the same time no doubt the charcoal burner would have to pay for the coppice timber used – about 14 tons for each burn apparently. The monks of Furness accepted the agricultural practice and the land tenure system of feudal times and worked within it. This involved too the restricted conditions of the human situation. Yet it would appear that they were not unmindful of their tenants' interests in return for their feudal obligations. Freeholders were exempt from tithes and the burgesses of Dalton were only charged 3/4d. on the burgage and provided only 6 men for the defence of the Abbey. Tenants were given free barrels of beer with 12 loaves to each barrel, they were given dung to enable them to manure fields, were provided with free meals in the Abbey and their children were given schooling. As is stated in the Victoria County History[6] "the isolation of Furness together with the supremacy of the Abbey gave that independence of tenure which has been so characteristic of the district. The villeins rose out of their servile condition easily". Contiguous with this land owned by the Abbey of Furness was that owned by the Augustinians of Cartmel Priory, granted to them by William Marshall, Earl of Pembroke in 1185 or 6. This covered the area between the Leven and Winster rivers and so bringing the whole of Lancashire north of the Sands under the ownership of religious houses. Cartmel too came to own large estates in Ireland – the Clare estates in Leinster, the Vill of Kilrush in Kildare with the advowson of its church, the church of Balbysare and chapel of Ballymaden in the diocese of Kildare. In addition there was property at Hest Bank and Bolton-le-Sands, with fishing rights on Haweswater, a moiety of the vill of Silverdale and a pension from the rectory at Whittington. So, as in the case of Furness, Cartmel extended her influence well beyond the area of the original endowment. Its centre was of course the parish church of Cartmel (The Priory) and it had chapels, including that of St. Anthony at Cartmel Fell. Presumably because of its position, it had the obligation to provide guides for the crossing of the sands of both the Kent and Leven estuaries, which it will be recalled had been the main route into Cartmel and Furness since Roman times, and which was to continue to be so until the middle of the nineteenth century.

Cartmel never achieved the eminence of Furness, but it had the distinction of being the only monastic building left intact at the Dissolution on the plea that it was the parish church. Today we see Cartmel Priory church pretty much as it was in medieval times.

Both Cartmel and Furness are typical examples of lowland monasteries in Cumbria and in the main can be taken to represent the situation land holding wise as well as economically of Carlisle Priory, Holm Cultram, Conishead and Lanercost. The only abbey in the upland region was that of Shap, founded in 1166, situated in a lonely and isolated site on the banks of the River Lowther about 1 mile from Shap village. As a community of the Premonstratensian Order (founded at Premontre in northern France in the early twelfth century by the German St. Norbert) whose monks were bound to personal poverty and austerity, the site in the narrow valley hidden from view was appropriate. It is unfortunate that most of its records are lost, but its endowments included the valley of Wet Sleddale, the village of Reagill and the estate of Milburn Grange, near Appleby, formerly owned by the monks of Holm Cultram. Its spiritual possessions were the churches of Shap, Warcop and Bampton. It would be interesting to know something of the agriculture practiced on the exposed Shap uplands (if any), more suitable for grazing than for cultivation and probably outside the enclosed field system except in the Appleby area of the upper Eden valley.

But Shap was not typical of the religious houses of Cumbria except in one particular: all ministered to the people through the churches which they controlled and more will be said of this in the section on parishes. Since the religious houses were such large landowners, the monks were intimately concerned with the lives of the people living in their lands. The Cistercians particularly were also interested in agriculture and it was in that sphere that they found common cause with their tenants. Manual work was an essential ingredient of the monastic way of life. Thus the religious houses became important elements in the secular life of their regions, and were as keen as anyone else to reap the benefits of the soil and take advantage of their position wherever possible. This is illustrated by the following extracts from the account of the Inglewood Forest "Eyre of William de Vesey, 1285, the Great Roll of Pleas of the Forest Nov. 3rd 1285"[7] (The Eyre was the court held about every 20 years to see to the business of the King's forest).

(a) The Prior of Wederhall (Wetheral) was ordered to fill in a dyke he had made as "it is in the King's demesne soil and nuisance to the forest . . . let him be in mercy and the dyke filled up".

(b) "The Bishop of Carlisle's men in Dalston, Condurak, Cartheu, Hawkesdal and of the Holme graze the land of Willeton, Warnhill, Great Rosseleye

7 C. & W.A.A.S., n.s., x.

and Little Rosseleye to the wastage of the herbage per annum of £4 since the last Eyre. The sum for that time is therefore £92. For which the men of the said township will answer."

(c) "The Abbot of Holme has his studs in the forest of Allerdale throughout the whole extent between Caldew and Ellen and the number is four score and upwards whereby the pasture of the deer is much overburdened. And because it is found that the Abbot had his studs there by the King's charter, therefore let him have them duly and in peace."

(d) Adam, Prior of Carlisle and the canons of the same house claim to have in the King's forest of Inglewood these liberties as follows: namely that the said prior and the canons claim for themselves and in right of their church at Carlisle common pasture for themselves and their men of their entire holding residing within the forest, throughout the entire forest in the King's demesne woods, except in the fence land, for all manner of their beasts. And they claim to have the whole tithe of venison taken within the forest of Inglewood so they should have that tithe of deer taken; that is to say the beast entire with the hide when it occurs; and they claim to have tithe of hay, of pannage, after pannage and agistment, of foals, calves, lambs, swine, goats, and all other beasts throughout the king's demesne in the forest aforesaid.

And they claim to have the tithe of all manner of fish caught in the lake of Ternwathelon (Tarn Wadling) which is called Laykebrayt and they claim to have the hides of all kinds of deer found dead throughout the forest in the forest aforesaid. And they claim to course hare and fox with their own dogs outside the covert; and they claim to have charcoal burners for making charcoal from dead wood lying on the grass wheresoever it be in the King's demesne wood for their own use. And they claim to have oaks blown down by the wind, if they or their men come upon them before others do so, for their own use, on marking such oaks with their axes as far as the heart of the oak.

They say that they have used (these privileges) from the olden times by custom and their possession exercised up till now from time out of mind. Further they produced a certain horn of ivory from their lord Henry, once King of England their founder, who had give them these liberties with that horn they had."

(Apparently the King (Edward I) was asked to adjudicate on this and found in favour of the abbot except for the blown down oak trees.)

The story of religious organisation apart from the parishes is not quite complete. During the early part of the thirteenth century the province of Umbria in Italy was the birthplace of the Order of Minor Friars (the Franciscans) a group dedicated to poverty and missionary work. Francis died in 1226 and was canonised two years later, but by then his work was well established and the first of the friars were introduced into the Carlisle Diocese by Bishop Mauclerk in 1223. They were in effect itinerant preachers who nevertheless lived to a religious rule. Carlisle itself saw both Dominican Friars and Franciscan Friars while in 1281 the Carmelite Friars were established in Appleby and in 1300 the Austin Friars were in Penrith. Their role would appear to be paralleled in the twentieth century by the Salvation Army. As a body they were devout and devoted doing their work of evangelism amongst, and giving succour to, the poorest and most neglected class of the population. Another group of religious men were the Hospitallers. Originally they were part of a military order founded to protect pilgrims to the sacred places in the Holy Land, becoming known as the Knights of St. John of Jerusalem. The Hospitallers were the Nursing Order of the Knights and as time went on and the Crusades came to an end they continued their activities westwards via Rhodes and Malta to Western Europe. In Cumbria they set up hospitals at Carlisle, Wigton, Kendal(e) and Kirkby Lonsdale.

The second way in which consolidation of the religious life of Cumbria occurred was through the development within the framework of episcopal organisation of the parochial system, a system which survives to this day in the Church of England. It is thought that prior to the coming of the Normans 'parishes' were not defined in territorial terms with specific boundary lines, for the churches which did exist were for the most part adjuncts of the manor, built by the lord of the manor and with a sphere of influence to include the settlement round it. The inhabitants were obliged to attend Mass and so long as the settlements were compact and the number of people relatively few, no great problems of distance occurred. But after about 1100 conditions were changing fairly rapidly and this somewhat casual arrangement could not continue. It is astonishing that the Diocese of Carlisle and part of the Archdeaconry of Richmond in Westmorland and Lancashire north of the Sands developed as it did in view of the problems it faced in the territorial, economic and political fields.

It will be recalled that Cumberland was too remote from Durham and York for effective control hence the creation of the Carlisle Diocese yet within the diocese itself remoteness existed and perhaps it would be better expressed in the term 'difficulty of access'. There is no doubt that the eventual distribution of parishes had its roots in the territorial framework of Celtic and later Anglo-Saxon Britain; the hundred, the tithing, the soke, for example, so that the progress towards the fixing of parish boundaries was evolutionary and over a long period. It is said that the parish system was rooted in the English soil by 1200. If it is so, then it can also be said that the original parishes in Cumbria (see Map 15) reflect quite closely the human geography of the area prior to the Norman Conquest. In the first chapter two aspects of the pre-Norman geography of Cumbria were mentioned – first the remoteness and isolation of the core, or the dome of the Lake District mountains, and second the prevalence of forest in the lower lying areas. Initially therefore the diocese and the southern areas were very unevenly populated with the majority living in the peripheral areas: West coast area, Solway Plain, Lower and Upper Eden valleys, the area around the Eamont, the Morecambe Bay area and the lower Lune valley. These areas were not too difficult of access and it was here that the largest number of parishes occurred since the acquisition of parish status depended largely on the number of inhabitants. As time went on and movement into the dome area occurred – largely helped by the monastic influences, the parishes on the periphery of the dome absorbed the higher lands. In the actual Lake District only three parishes existed – Bampton, Crosthwaite (Keswick) and Bassenthwaite. All the western dales were in St. Bees Parish, all the southern ones in Millom or Dalton, the eastern in Kendal(e), Bampton, Shap, Barton or Greystoke and the northern dales in Brigham, Crosthwaite and Bassenthwaite. Thus there came to be a gradation in the size of parishes; the smallest in area were those round the lower Eden valley and Carlisle, those on the west coast between the Derwent and the Duddon and those in the middle and upper Eden basin. These areas represent very closely the areas of religious activity in the Celtic and Anglian periods. The largest parishes were those which included the area of the core, illustrated by those of St. Bees in the west and Kendal(e) in the south. St. Bees stretched from the coast as far inland as Ennerdale, Loweswater, Wasdale and Eskdale, covering well over 200 square miles. Kendal(e) was almost as big until Grasmere and Windermere were granted parochial status, and even then it was something like 150 square miles in extent. Since burials could only take place at the mother church no wonder that corpse roads were necessary in the hilly areas. Map 22 shows something of the gradations of size from the lower to the higher land. Note also the few parishes covering the extensive uplands of the Pennines to the east of the Eden valley. So problems of population density in relation to the height of the land and accessibility was one influencing factor in parish formation. But more important and indirectly related to the first point was the economic factor. During this period the region was essentially agricultural economically speaking and the prevailing feudal system determined the size and type of settlement possible. Coupled with this and complementary to it was the land use pattern set by the monasteries. A third element also played its part. Much of the lower land was forested, and one of the forests, that of Inglewood was a 'Royal Forest' which restricted development in a number of ways. Each of these factors needs to be dealt with.

The lowland areas of the Solway in the north-west and west of the region presented problems for agriculture. Large areas were badly drained and in parts the surface was of heavy blue clay which tended to be baked hard in dry weather and become waterlogged during the rains in winter. The badly drained areas gave a peaty surface. It was on the drumlins and pockets of higher boulder clay that dry fertile soils were found. Fortunately, the ice age left a fairly large number of such possible sites for settlement and the result was a series of nucleated villages – the nucleation being associated with the manorial system. It is perhaps not relevant to go into details of the system of farming except to say that the most common pattern was the single open field system, as opposed to the two or three field systems farther south in England. This open field, often surrounding the village with its manor and church, was divided into two – the in field and the out field, the former being cropped every year and therefore needing heavy manuring, and the latter divided into years of cropping and years of fallow depending on the quality of the soils; usually the pattern was five years cropping and five years fallow or three years cropping and nine years fallow. This field was land cleared of trees. On the perimeter was the waste land which was usually much more extensive than the cultivated area. Presumably it was on this waste area where the final parish boundaries were drawn. In addition hamlets sprang up where, although poor in quality the land could be used for grazing. These hamlets would have to rely on the nearer villages for subsistence and perhaps could be compared with the granges of the monasteries, dealt with elsewhere. The important thing is that this type of boundary favoured pastoralism which became the mainstay of the agricultural economy of Cumbria. Weather conditions with a high rainfall precluded much wheat growing and oats was the staple crop. Crop rotations were designed to give the maximum amount of grazing particularly during the winter months to obviate the necessity of too much autumn slaughtering which was a common feature before the agricultural revolution of the seventeenth and eighteenth centuries, when the introduction of root crops allowed for winter feed. From March to September the stock, sheep and cattle were grazed on this waste, during the autumn they grazed the stubble of the open field and in winter they were housed and fed on meadow hay (very limited in amount).

In Cumberland the farming tradition was already a pastoral one in which the relatively small open fields were integrated into the system of stock husbandry, based primarily on the large common waste. This type of farming with its associated and either nucleated or 'street' village pattern was largely responsible for the shape and size of the parishes wherever it was practiced. It also as time went on associated itself with the pastoral land use of the dome although the system of farming carried out by the monasteries tended to differ and it was the monastic development of the 'dome' which was paramount.

The other area of considerable cultivation was that of the middle and upper Eden valley and of the Eamont and Lowther valleys. Here again the soil was not particularly fertile, being light and sandy, with the result that as in the Solway area, pastoralism prevailed, with less number of open fields and more waste. Further east on the Pennine slopes there was seasonal grazing – an early form of transhumance.

It is reckoned that by the fifteenth century there were 288 townships in Cumberland of which 220 had open fields mainly in the lowland areas, but as G. Elliott[8] points out "Before 1500 they (open fields) were still growing in the area, as the waste was actively reclaimed in response to the stimuli of an increasing rural population and an added demand for human and stock food".

The great period for enclosure in this area was not yet. So these agricultural villages, the focal points in the feudal manorial system, became the parishes of the Church. Initially it was the manor which was the recognised territorial division, the civic centre of the local

[8] G. Elliott, 'The system of Cultivation and evidence of enclosures in the Cumberland open fields in the 16th century', C.&W.A.A.S., n.s., lix.

community, but during feudal times the parish replaced the manor and the church the manor house, with the result that manorial court rents and tithes were paid at the church and at it too land was sold and conveyed. From this time onwards for some hundreds of years the church became the centre of both the religious and secular life. It became also the centre of the social and cultural life.

With increasing economic activities came increased trade, with the necessary increase in merchants and markets – distribution centres for agricultural produce and for the other necessities of life. This kind of activity required permission from the Crown and charters for the holding of markets came to be granted to key centres, centres which were accessible within Cumbria and also accessible to places elsewhere, or places which held a key geographical position in defence. The establishment of market towns was of tremendous significance in the country as a whole as well as in Cumbria. The manorial system produced a rural population with an upper class (the lord of the manor and landowners) and a lower class (the workers), but the development of the market towns saw the emergence of an urban population in which the middle class (merchants, professional people, etc.) played an increasingly important part. It was these three social classes which were to determine the future course of the Church. In Cumbria, market towns developed mainly during the thirteenth century and give a good clue to the distribution of population. The following are the towns concerned, with the dates of the respective charters for holding markets: Kendal(e), 1189; Kirkoswald, 1201; Ravenglass, 1208; Penrith, 1221/2; Kirkby Lonsdale, Cockermouth, 1227; Millom, 1234; Ireby, 1237; Carlisle, Appleby and Brampton, 1250; Kirkambeck, 1251; Wigton, 1262; Egremont, 1267; Keswick, 1276; Flookburgh 1278; Ulverston, Seaton, 1280; Brough, 1284; Dalton, 1292; Cartmel, 1292, to be followed in the fourteenth century by Skinburness, Bootle and Kirkby Stephen (see Map 1). It will be noticed that not all these were parishes in their own right during this period.

So by the end of the feudal system and the beginning of the Tudor dynasty, the secular and religious framework of the countryside had been established.

One other aspect of the geography of the area needs to be considered. As already said, the lowland areas were well covered with trees and in Cumbria was one royal forest, that of Inglewood. The word forest used in this connection was a legal term and not a botanical one. Much of a forest was woodland, although clearings existed for settlement. A royal forest was a preserve owned by the King and outside common law, administered by a special code known as 'forest law'. Its object was to safeguard the king's hunting, to preserve deer and wild boar and the timber which gave them shelter. Thus stringent rules were in operation to this end and accounts of the courts or 'eyres' which occurred at intervals, give an interesting insight into what happened within them (see p. 48).

These extracts tell something of activity within the forest, but they also illustrate the growing influence of the religious houses and their economic importance. They were becoming privileged in the material sense and of course as stated earlier were acquiring great wealth through the acquisition of land.

The forest of Inglewood covered about 150 square miles stretching south from Carlisle for about 16 miles, between the Calder and Petteril rivers approaching Greystoke in the south and the Eden in the east. It is clear that farming took place within the confines of the forest with enclosures in clearings where hamlets and villages were to be found. However T. H. B. Graham points out[9] "A church situate within the forest did not properly possess a parish because all the unenclosed land belonged to the king and was extra parochial". Strict rules concerning such things as grazing rights (pannage) and the clearing of woodland to enable cultivation to be carried on (assarting) meant that the population within the forest was kept low with a fairly even spread throughout the area. The result of this was that parishes were relatively few in number and of large size, a situation still existing today. Moreover villages were few and settlements were mainly of the hamlet type.

Inglewood had 4 verderers to see that the rules were kept, under the jurisdiction of a Warden or chief administration officer, which was a hereditary post held by the barony of Burgh-by-Sands.

Two other forests existed, those of Allerdale and Copeland, and while they were not strictly speaking 'royal' forests they were sanctuaries for game and were more appropriately called chases. Here too there were restrictions although as in the case of Inglewood the commoners had certain rights, e.g. to collect fuel, to dig peat, to pasture pigs at the harvest time etc. From the geographical point of view then

[9] T. H. B. Graham, 'The Medieval Diocese of Carlisle', C. & W.A.A.S., n.s., xxv.

the development of the church during the period from the Norman conquest to roughly the dissolution of the monasteries·must be seen against the background of the feudal system of territorial divisions, the rise and fall of the monasteries and religious houses, both secular and regular, and the over-riding authority of the King as seen in the 'royal' forests. These in turn were influenced by the physical geography of Cumbria with its large upland component and its isolated position in relation to the rest of the country and its weather conditions. All these are reflected in the economic expansion and the development of communications, still to be dealt with.

Before dealing directly with the church in the light of this geographical background a digression to an aspect of history cannot be ignored. As the *Victoria County History* states, "For almost three centuries from this date (1296) the history of the diocese owing to Scottish invasions is coloured by the troubles and devastations arising from its geographical position". The border nature of Cumbria has already been mentioned and from the time of the early church to that of the union between England and Scotland in 1603, there was trouble from Scottish invaders. It will be recalled that until 1157 Scotland laid claim to Cumbria and occupied it on a number of occasions, and after 1157 Scots raiders repeatedly advanced through the region, looting, pillaging and particularly stealing stock and driving them back over the border. No part of Cumbria escaped their incursions and it is astonishing that any progress of a permanent nature was made. Obviously the church suffered, yet in spite of all, survived and grew in stature (see p. 61).

A brief summary of Scottish incursions after 1157 will illustrate the problem:

    1173, 1174, 1215 – Raids on and sieges of Carlisle.
    1216 – Holm Cultram Abbey pillaged.
    1296 – The Earl of Buchan raided Cumberland. Lanercost Priory burned.
    1301 – Destruction of a large part of the diocese of Carlisle, Monasteries pillaged.
    1314 – Calder Priory destroyed, incursion up Eden valley, Brough and Appleby burnt.
    1315 – Lord James Douglas besieged Carlisle, went through the plain of Cumberland. St. Bees Priory destroyed, Egremont attacked, Calder Priory damaged.

1316 – Furness area raided and ravaged.

1318 – Looting and pillaging on border.

1322 – Army of Robert Bruce ravaged Allerdale, Coupland and Cumberland generally. Manor of Rose burnt, Cartmel Priory desolated (Furness Abbey saved by paying a ransom), Holm Cultram plundered.

1345 – Penrith burnt.

1380/90 – Carlisle besieged four times.

1402 – Border raids.

1430/40 – More border raids.

1468/70 – More border skirmishing with pillaging.

1542 – Destruction in the Solway region; pillaging and ravaging.

Add to these the effect of the Wars of the Roses in the second half of the fifteenth century when the great families of Cumbria were divided in their loyalties, the Percies, Cliffords, Dacres and Greystokes for the Lancastrian cause and the Huddlestons (Millom) and Stricklands for the Yorkists, and one can sympathise with both the secular and religious authorities in their efforts to carry out their responsibilities.

The development of the Diocese of Carlisle and that part of Cumbria in the Archdeaconry of Richmond was very much influenced by the environmental facts already described, but in trying to unravel some of the complexities of parish affairs particularly from the financial point of view and the system of appointments to benefices it is clear that many of the problems were created from within the church itself. The maintenance of the churches and the emoluments of the priests was built on the customs from very early Christian times – ecclesiastical patronage and glebe land, but it had to be modified to fit into the feudal system, and as the parochial system developed the granting of land, or the gift of it, the endowing of churches etc. appears to have been at the whim of individuals from the King downwards, resulting in a quite haphazard system in which the strong (e.g. the monastic houses) become stronger and more wealthy, while the weak became weaker and poorer (e.g. the parish priest). The constant incursions of the Scottish raiders made matters worse so that for instance in 1301 Bishop Halton of Carlisle could write "Some of the religious were scattered as their monasteries were destroyed and several of the churches with their parishes were reduced to ashes insomuch that the clergy were unable to live off the fruits of their benefices but were forced to beg alms from place to place".[10] And the same bishop begged the Pope to sanction the

[10] See *V.C.H., Cumberland*, vol. 2.

appropriation of the church of Horncastle in Lincolnshire in order to increase his revenues.

But to return to the creation of the Diocese of Carlisle in 1133. Initially Henry I endowed it with valuable rectories in Derbyshire and Lincolnshire – a safer source of income perhaps than land near the border and from then onwards the various bishops acquired more and more property as occasion allowed. In 1301 Bishop Halton got the rectories of Dalston, Rothbury and Horncastle, Bishop Mauclerk having been granted the Manor of Dalston for the bishop's residence in 1230. He it was who purchased the soke of Horncastle and acquired a house in London. From the above it will be seen that the church respected no boundaries and as Carlisle obtained land revenue from elsewhere in the kingdom so land in Cumberland went to bodies outside. Torpenhow was granted to Holyrood Abbey in Edinburgh, Lazonby parish gave a pension to the Abbot of Kelso while in the reverse direction Holm Cultram Abbey was endowed from Galloway. Fountains and Byland Abbeys owned land in Cumberland as did St. Mary's York in Kendale, Westmorland. These interchanges were taking place at the same time as the religious houses were acquiring land and all started with the arrival of the Normans and the granting of land by the Crown, as has been previously stated, and it was the barons as well as the Crown who caused the confusion, almost a scramble. The Normans were Christian militants and it was they who made it possible for the golden age of monasticism in the twelfth century and for the great power of the church in the thirteenth and fourteenth centuries.

But the grass roots of Christianity were in the parish churches, and here the story is of constant shortages of clergy and of their poverty. The cause to a considerable degree was the economic instability of the area through its border position and the constant burning, looting and pillaging of the Scottish marauders. This had a chain effect and it was the parish clergy who suffered most – it was a case of passing the buck. Under the feudal system the local priest was entitled to a fixed proportion of the cultivated area of the village – a legacy of the private church of the lord of the manor in pre-Norman days – usually a double portion compared with the other members of the community, and in return he had to provide the male animals to service the herds and flocks. This was the beginning of the parson's freehold in England. In addition tithes were paid, usually representing 1/10th of the 'fruits of the earth'. Originally the tithe had gone to the 'Mother Church' or 'Baptismal Church', but as time went on there was increasing pressure to have it attached to specific churches or benefices from whose community it was derived. The lord of the manor, and later the bishops claimed a percentage of church dues and offerings, and as landlords, were patrons of livings with power to choose an incumbent. An incumbent so chosen became entitled to the income derived as above, plus any endowments previously given by the pious to the parish, plus any rent for land owned by the church as a result of gifts. Thus a rector could become a wealthy person in a parish which was well endowed and in a fertile area. But power corrupts and in course of time individuals acquired more than one benefice and the system of pluralities came into being – even bishops were not immune as shown when Bishop Halton (1292-1324) acquired the rectories of Dalston, Rothbury and Horncastle (Lincolnshire) while at one stage in the fifteenth century one man held the livings of Melmerby, Lazonby and Dufton. A stipendiary priest was appointed to look after the cure of souls at a cheaper price in those churches necessarily having an absentee rector.

The term 'appropriation' has already been mentioned. This was the system whereby the patron of a living gave the benefice to a religious house or to the diocese thus transferring the assets to a corporate body. It is reckoned that nearly half the parish churches in England changed hands in this way and Cumbria was no exception. In all, 26 appropriations were made, 13 in Carlisle Diocese and 13 in the Archdeaconry of Richmond. Revenue was thus taken away from the local churches and a stipendiary priest appointed by the new 'owners'. This naturally deprived many parishes of endowments and other sources of income. During the thirteenth century attempts were made probably to counteract this deprivation, to institute the system of vicarages whereby a priest was appointed to a parish with a definite stipend and security of tenure. Bishop Grosseteste of Lincoln was the instigator of this.

This type of development in the structure of the church had grave consequences in Cumbria, for it was happening during the period of the Scottish raids when much of the value of land and property was constantly being lowered. The nadir appears to have been in the early part of the fourteenth century, when the value of temporalities and spiritualities in the diocese of Carlisle dropped from £3,171 5s. 7½d. in

1292 to £480 19s. 0d. in 1318. The Papal Taxation totals illustrate this even more dramatically.

Papal Taxation	in 1291			in 1318[11]		
Diocese of Carlisle – Religious Houses	£	s.	d.	£	s.	d.
The Bishopric	126	7	0	20	0	0
Carlisle	96	19	0	20	0	0
Shap	46	13	4	2	0	0
Armathwaite	10	0	0	—		
Lanercost	74	12	$6\frac{1}{2}$	—		
Wetheral	52	17	6	4	0	0
Holm Cultram	206	5	10	40	0	0
Archdeaconry of Richmond						
Cartmel	21	11	8	3	6	8
Conishead	9	0	0	1	10	0
St. Bees	12	9	3	3	6	8
Calder	32	0	0	5	0	0
Furness	176	0	0	13	6	8

The total income of the Diocese of Carlisle incumbents fell from £1,616 17s. 5d. in 1292 to £1,201 16s. 0d. in 1535 (the end of the medieval period) while that of incumbents in the Archdeaconry of Richmond fell from £810 13s. 6d. to £461 12s. 11d. Efforts were made to recoup some of these losses, hence such changes as appropriations and pluralities, for instance in 1332 Holm Cultram Abbey obtained the church of Wigton "in consideration of great losses due to Scots forays" and Bishop Halton begged for Horncastle to secure more income and be a possible refuge in times of trouble. In 1302 Bishop Halton had to reduce tithes and in some cases cancel them altogether. The net result of all this was that throughout the period there was a great shortage of clergy and considerable poverty among those that existed. Bishops repeatedly complained about this and altogether the parochial clergy worked under great difficulties. In 1337 for instance the bishop was complaining that he could not obtain any tithes because all the clergy had fled.

R. S. Ferguson states of Cumberland in 1536 "Their clergy were probably the most ignorant in England and the people were probably content with them."[12] A not very flattering picture!

[11] C. M. L. Bouch, *Prelates and People of the Lake Counties* (Kendal, 1948).

[12] R. S. Ferguson, *A History of Cumberland* (County History Reprints), (S.R. Pub., 1970).

A third element contributed to this depressing story. During the fourteenth century there were a series of plagues starting with the Black Death in 1348 and further ones in 1361 and 1369. Bishops were again complaining about the shortage of clergy.

Is it not surprising that in spite of all the difficulties the church continued to grow in strength. The period began with much church building, there being today 60 churches in the Carlisle diocese with evidence of twelfth-century work, the Normans apparently being very dissatisfied with what they found and of course used stone as opposed to timber for some of the Anglian churches. It also ended with a flourish of building in the late fifteenth and early sixteenth centuries, at a time when the Scottish raids were over and a more stable life was possible.

By 1540 it is clear, the parochial system was firmly established within the hierarchy of the episcopy in spite of the many difficulties resulting from the border position of the See of Carlisle, the secular power of the barons and the secular and religious power of the monasteries. Yet perhaps not in spite of the barons and monastic houses but because of them. The feudal system preserved the status quo rather than destroyed it and it suited the monasteries to fit into that pattern. It was not the border situation that primarily determined the distribution of parishes or the diocesan organisation resulting from that distribution, but a combination of history and geography. Geographically speaking the following factors have emerged so far. The relative isolation of this area from the rest of England produced an independence reflected in the establishing of the See of Carlisle while historical tradition proved stronger in the south with Furness, Cartmel, Coupland and the barony of Kendale remaining in the York diocese. The mountainous central area of Cumbria with its radial system of drainage, the marshes of part of the coastal lowland, particularly in the Solway area, the considerable areas of woodland, including the king's preserve in the Forest of Inglewood all played their part in the distribution of settlements and thus of parishes – restricting them in the main to the river valleys and the lower land on the periphery. These geographical influences had been at work throughout the whole of the Christian era and the position ecclesiastically speaking by 1540 was the result of an evolutionary process compounded of not only geographical factors, but also of the imponderables of history.

So to sum up. The position in 1541 was as follows:

The Diocese of Carlisle was centred on Carlisle itself in the priory church of St. Mary, in 1541 becoming the Cathedral Church of the Holy and Undivided Trinity, with the Bishops established at Rose Castle in the parish of Dalston, south of the city. The Archdeacon of Carlisle had responsibility for the whole of the Diocese divided into four deaneries, those of Carlisle, Allerdale, Westmorland (part) and Cumberland stretching from the Scottish border in the north to Ullswater and the middle Eden valley in the south, from the west coast and the River Derwent in the west to the Pennine watershed in the east. In all there were 91 parishes, the only difference from those of the original diocese being the addition of Newton Arlosh and the decay and disappearance of Eston, Cambok, and Carlaton. The distribution of these 91 parishes illustrates the points previously made. There is a concentration along the valley and estuary of the River Eden, another on the lower lands of the Solway linked with the drumlin distribution of higher points – mainly dry point sites, and almost a complete lack in the mountainous interior.

The parishes with their Deaneries were:

Parishes in the Carlisle Diocese (listed in 1291) (in alphabetical order)

Carlisle Deanery
Aikton, Arthuret, Beaumont, Bewcastle, Bowness-on-Solway, Brampton, Burgh-by-Sands, Cambok,* Carlaton,* Carlisle (St. Cuthbert), Castle Carrock, Crosby-on-Eden, Cumrew, Cumwhitton, Dalston, Denton, Eston,* Farlam, Great Orton, Grinsdale, Hayton, Irthington, Kirkandrews-on-Eden, Kirkbampton, Kirklinton, Rockcliffe, Scaleby, Sebergham, Stanwix, Stapleton, Thursby, Walton, Wetheral.
(*Decayed)

Allerdale Deanery
Aspatria, Bassenthwaite, Bolton, Bridekirk, Bromfield, Caldbeck, Camerton, Cross Canonby, Crosthwaite, Dearham, Gilcrux, Ireby, Isel, Kirkbride, Plumbland, Torpenhow, Uldale, Wigton.

Westmorland Deanery
Appleby St. Lawrence, Appleby St. Michael, Asby, Askham, Bampton, Barton, Brougham, Brough-under-Stainmore, Cliburn, Clifton, Crosby Garrett, Crosby Ravensworth, Dufton, Kirkby Stephen, Kirkby Thore, Long Marton, Lowther, Morland, Musgrave, Newbiggin, Ormside, Orton, Ravenstonedale, Shap, Warcop.

Cumberland Deanery
Addingham, Ainstable, Castle Sowerby, Croglin, Dacre, Edenhall, Great Salkeld, Greystoke, Hutton-in-the-Forest, Kirkland, Kirkoswald, Lazonby, Melmerby, Ousby, Penrith, Renwick, Skelton.

That part in the Diocese of York was under the jurisdiction of the Archdeaconry of Richmond, a relic of the days before the Counties and their boundaries were established. The parishes in 1541 numbered 37, and were divided into 4 deaneries – Kendale, Lonsdale, Furness and Coupland. The area covered by the 37 parishes was roughly the same as that for the 91 parishes of the Carlisle diocese and the significance of the resultant average size differences will be discussed later. The distribution shows a concentration along the the west coast of Cumberland (south of the River Derwent) and along the coastlands of the northern shores of Morecambe Bay in Lancashire. The upland areas of the Lakeland hills had few parishes.

The parishes with their Deaneries were:

Parishes in the Archdeaconry of Richmond (later Diocese of Chester) (listed 1291)

Coupland Deanery
Beckermet, Bootle, Brigham, Cleator, Corney, Dean, Distington, Egremont, Gosforth, Haile, Harrington, Irton, Lamplugh, Millom, Moresby, Muncaster, Ponsonby, St. Bees, Whicham, Whitbeck, Workington.

Furness Deanery
Aldingham, Cartmel, Dalton, Kirkby Ireleth, Pennington, Ulverston, Urswick.

Kendale Deanery
Beetham, Burton, Grasmere, Heversham, Kendal(e), Windermere.

Lonsdale Deanery
Kirkby Lonsdale.

A map (Map 15) of the parishes listed in the Papal Taxation returns of 1291 illustrates these.

It will be recalled that in the Middle Ages Cumbria was an area of small, compact agricultural settlements working within the framework of a feudal system. "A traveller in Tudor times would have seen small villages and hamlets, each surrounded by a few fields of cultivated land, with common adjoining, and then a waste stretching for miles until the next oasis of cultivation was reached and crossed, if at all, by rude and often hardly passable tracks".[13] During this period there was a degree of urbanisation with the development of trade and the setting up of market towns. Thus it can be assumed that while the total population

[13] C. M. L. Bouch & G. P. Jones, *The Lake Counties 1500-1830* (Manchester, 1961).

PARISHES LISTED IN PAPAL TAXATION RETURNS, 1291

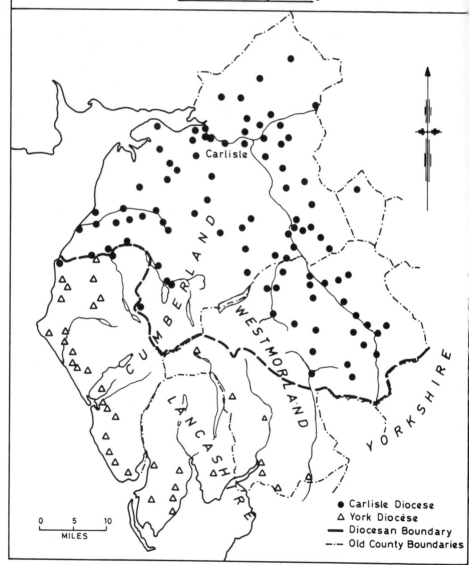

Carlisle

CUMBERLAND

WESTMORLAND

LANCASHIRE

YORKSHIRE

● Carlisle Diocese
△ York Diocese
━━ Diocesan Boundary
—·— Old County Boundaries

0   5   10
MILES

Map 15

was relatively small significant increases were taking place. In addition the religious houses had, in becoming landowners, penetrated further and further into the higher land to develop their sheep runs while at the same time increased productivity on their lower land possessions through more careful husbandry and such things as land reclamation through draining of marshes (of which a good example is Holm Cultram) forest clearances etc. Thus one would expect the density of population to increase in the lower traditional agricultural areas, while at the same time there would be a movement of people into the higher parts to form new settlements where the religious houses were particularly active. Demographically speaking then during this period there should be (a) an increase in and (b) a redistribution of population. It is interesting to note that the existing parishes remained static in numbers so how were the increased numbers to be catered for when church attendance was compulsory? The answer was by the building of chapels within the framework of existing parishes and served by them.

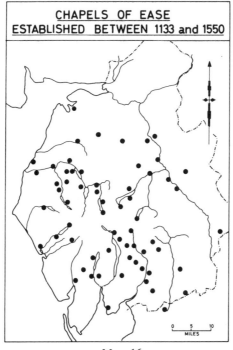

CHAPELS OF EASE
ESTABLISHED BETWEEN 1133 and 1550

Map 16

During this period something like 75 were consecrated and by 1600 a further 25 were added. Their distribution shows that they were concentrated in the upper reaches of the river valleys e.g. Derwent and Crake, extending well into the central dome (see Map 16). The list with dates of consecration and the parishes involved were:

Chapels consecrated prior to 1541

Diocese of Carlisle

Deaneries of Carlisle and Allerdale
Parish of St. Mary's, Carlisle – Armathwaite (ante 1401), Hesket-in-the-Forest (ante 1541), Langwathby (1302), Westward (1374)
Parish of Greystoke – Threlkeld (1225), Watermillock (ante 1230)
Parish of Crosthwaite – Borrowdale (1550)
Parish of Aspatria – Allhallows (1184)
Parish of Bassenthwaite – Bassenthwaite (1471)
Parish of Kirkland – Culgaith (1456)
Parish of Holm Cultram – Flimby (ante 1150), Newton Arlosh (1304)
Parish of Dalston – High Head or Ivegill (1358)
Parish of Penrith – Newton Reigny (1338)

Deanery of Cumberland
Parish of Brougham – St. Wilfrid (1200)
Parish of Morland – Bolton (pre-1540)
Parish of Kirkby Thore – Milburn (1227), Temple Sowerby (1227)
Parish of Barton – Martindale (ante-1247), Patterdale (1348)
Parish of Shap – Mardale (pre-1540)
Parish of Brough – Stainmore (1506)

Diocese of Chester (previously York) (see p. 69)
Deanery of Coupland
Parish of St. Bees – Ennerdale (1534), Eskdale (1445), Loweswater (1125), Nether Wasdale (1535)
Parish of Brigham – Cockermouth (1221), Embleton (1210), Lorton (1198), Buttermere (1507), Setmurthy (1225)
Parish of Workington – Clifton (1181)
Parish of Gosforth – Drigg (1170)

Deanery of Furness
Parish of Cartmel – Cartmel Fell (1540), Flookburgh (1520)
Parish of Dalton – Hawkshead (1200) (given parochial rights)
Parish of Hawkshead – Colton (1530)
Parish of Ireleth – Broughton-in-Furness (ante-1547), Woodland (ante-1550)
Parish of Ulverston – Lowick (1292), Torver (1338)

Deanery of Lonsdale
Parish of Kirkby Lonsdale – Barbon (pre-1540), Hutton Roof (pre-1540), Killington (pre-1540)

Deanery of Kendale
Parish of Kendal(e) – Burneside (pre-1540), Crook (pre-1540), Grayrigg (ante-1469), Natland (1246), Old Hutton (1467), Selside (pre-1540), Kentmere (1453), Staveley (ante-1338), Winster (pre-1540)
Parish of Grasmere – Ambleside (ante-1494)
Parish of Heversham – Crosscrake (pre-1540)
Parish of Burton – Preston Patrick (1331)

Others not attached to parishes were also consecrated during this period including 7 in the Holm Cultram area, 3 at Cockermouth, 3 at Wigton, and one each at Waverton, Papcastle and Braithwaite.

Between 1541 and 1600 there were further chapels including those at St. John's-in-the-Vale (1554), Keswick (1554), Wythburn (1554), all in the Parish of Crosthwaite; Wasdale Head (1552) in the Parish of St. Bees; Wythop (1552), Mosser (1547), in the Parish of Brigham; Ings (1546), Underbarrow (1547), Skelsmergh (1578), Witherslack in the parish of Kendal(e); Longdale (1571), Long Sleddale in Grasmere parish.

By 1541 the parish of Kendal(e) was responsible for 9 chapels with 2 further ones to come by 1560. Already two of the chapels – Windermere and Grasmere had received full parochial status (in 1348 and 1349 respectively) with the consecration of graveyards. But as has already been said this was unusual and came about because of the obvious difficulties of distance and weather conditions for all burials to take place at the mother church. Incumbents were averse to shedding any of their parochial rights as Bouch points out.[14]

"Transition from chapelry to parish seems to have been increasingly difficult, perhaps because of the hardening of vested interests, since the grant of parochial rights to a chapel meant the loss of valuable fees to the incumbent of the mother church."

The religious houses would also be a strong reason for little basic change.

The assumptions about population distribution and therefore the demographic factors involved in parish and chapel distribution can only be justified if the facts support them.

There is no means of knowing any precise population statistics, but evidence of economic development, demanding more workers is available. Between 1127 and 1200 the monks of Furness brought 2,000

[14] C. M. L. Bouch, *Prelates and People of the Lake Counties* (Kendal, 1948).

acres of arable land into cultivation and by 1250 were using 1,400 acres in Upper Eskdale for sheep runs. At least 7 chapels were established in these areas. Furness Abbey also owned land in Borrowdale, shared with Fountains Abbey. This land was part of the parish of Crosthwaite which covered more than 70 square miles. During this period 5 chapels were in use. Sheep farming resulted in the woollen cloth industry and spinning galleries are a feature of some farms today. In 1453 there were 6 fulling mills in Grasmere, by 1500 there were 18.

While mining was still in its infancy there was nevertheless some activity in the getting of copper, silver and lead, as well as iron.

All this implied trade, which originally was routed through the monasteries, but as time went on the market towns became the foci, as for example Kendal(e) as the main centre for woollen cloth, the famous "Kendal Green".

This is not very sound evidence to support the earlier contention of an increasing population, and it must be admitted that in the early years of the sixteenth century Cumbria was thinly populated compared with some other parts of England. It is reckoned that at that time there were about 70-80,000 inhabitants in Cumbria (Cumberland 45,000 and Westmorland 25,000 plus) with the rest being in the Lancashire area north of the Sands. Thus 1/50th of the total population of the country lived in 1/20th of the national acreage. The density of population varied enormously in different parts of the region from about 70 per square mile in places like Appleby to 18 in the central core parishes such as Crosthwaite.

CHAPTER 4
1540-1640 The Post-Reformation Church

The year 1541 was important in the religious life of Cumbria. In that year (Aug. 4th) the Diocese of Chester was created and the Archdeaconry of Richmond was included in it – that is the part of Cumberland south of the Derwent (Coupland), the barony of Kendale in Westmorland along with the Cartmel and Furness areas – the first Bishop being John Bird, suffragan to the Bishop of Llandaff. This was the situation for the next 300 years. In 1541 there was a change in the organisation of the Carlisle diocese. Until then the cathedral was also the priory church of St. Mary, but with the dissolution of the religious houses the priory ceased to function and a charter was given for the church to become the Cathedral Church of the Holy and Undivided Trinity.

These two changes marked the end of the medieval period and the beginning of a new era which saw the emergence of the Church of England as we know it today and the renunciation of all papal authority. For twenty years at least until the Act of Supremacy and the Act of Uniformity of 1559 – much confusion occurred. Generally speaking the transition in the Carlisle diocese took place without a great deal of opposition but there is no doubt that the Church suffered greatly. Bouch[1] heads his chapter 1 in Book II The Sixteenth Century, "The Reformation or a Northern Tragedy", and goes on to quote from Miss R. Dodds[2] – "The north of England at the beginning of the sixteenth century was the poorer and most backward part of the kingdom, the part therefore, which required most attention and care at the hands of a competent ruler. So far Henry (VIII) had not done well by it. He found the north poor, and he robbed it of the only treasure it possessed in the wealth of the abbeys. He found it backward and he nearly destroyed the only civilising influence at work there, the Church. He found that the people cherished among many faults, a few rude

[1] C. M. L. Bouch, *Prelates and People of the Lake Counties*, (Kendal, 1948).
[2] M. H. & R. Dodds, *The Pilgrimage of Grace*.

virtues, truthfulness, personal honour, fidelity to family and friends. He made no serious efforts to reform their faults, but did his best to eradicate their virtues.'

It is not clear on what evidence she bases her comments on the character of the Cumbrians, but there is no doubt about the damage done to the church both by Henry VIII and his son Edward VI. This is not to imply that Cumbria was treated differently from any other part of the country but any deprivation had greater effect in an area already poor and backward. Much of the church property, and that of the religious houses was taken into secular control, and thus a considerable part of the church income was lost. The exception in Cumbria was the transfer of the endowments of Carlisle and Wetheral to the Dean and Chapter of Carlisle. For instance Edward VI seized lands and endowments of chantries, free chapels, stipendiary curacies and collegiate churches. The collegiate churches of Greystoke and Kirkoswald were dissolved in 1542. Edward also ordered the confiscation of plate and other valuables from all churches and their sale to enrich his coffers. Some of the wealth went to individuals such as Thomas Preston of Preston Patrick and Levens who was given the lease of Cartmel. Some went to corporations; Holm Cultram to Oxford University, Furness to the Duchy of Lancaster.

It would be remarkable if all these changes – including the changes in religious observance had been made without some dissent. The Pilgrimage of Grace in 1536/7 was symptomatic when some 15,000 men marched on Carlisle, later diverted to Cockermouth without achieving anything. Henry VIII ordered severe reprisals in Cumberland and Westmorland, 66 men were hanged in various villages.

The Bishops of Carlisle had constantly complained of lack of clergy in the diocese and of the quality of those in the parishes. These years saw little change. The plight of the clergy worsened and their numbers diminished still further, as the following figures show.

| | Numbers of Clergy | | |
	1524	*1548*	*1554*
Kendal(e)	47	33	24
Kirkby Lonsdale	7	11	8
Heversham	9	9	3
Windermere	5	5	3
Cockermouth	5	4	1

So by 1560 the state of the church left much to be desired, and leadership was lacking. This state seems to have persisted during the last quarter of the sixteenth century for in 1599 Bishop Robinson was complaining about the weakness and carelessness of the ministry and the shortage of clergy. Writing in 1599 to Cecil he wrote, "In the more peaceful parts of the diocese there are some clergymen of very commendable parts, both for knowledge and conscience, but their number is very small. Others there were that might do much good if they had half that delight in discharging their functions which they have in idleness, vain pleasure and worldly cares. The far greater number is utterly unlearned, unable to read English truly and distinctly."

It was perhaps inevitable that reaction to the Reformation should set in as time went on and under the surface Roman Catholicism persisted. People practising Roman Catholicism were known as recusants and Bishop Robinson writing to Secretary Cecil in 1599 stated, "I find here (Carlisle diocese) more popish recusants than I thought, yet the number within my diocese is far less than within the barony of Kendale and deanery of Copeland, in Cumberland, both belonging to the jurisdiction of Chester". This dissension to the new order in Church and State continued for many years, aggravated in the early years by the independence of the great families of Percy and Neville, the Earls of Northumberland and Westmorland respectively. It had reached its climax perhaps by about 1569 with open rebellion resulting in the defeat of the Earls and a strengthening of the Tudor dynasty.

It is reckoned that during the reign of Elizabeth I there were about 400 or 500 practising Roman Catholics in Cumbria, the leader being John Bost, the son of a Westmorland landowner, who was ordained at Douai in France in 1580. By 1593 there were 21 priests.

Meanwhile there were still some clergy within the Church of England who were unhappy with the New Prayer Book and the Thirty-Nine Articles to which they had to subscribe, and in the 1570s seven were deprived of their livings, at Dacre, Melmerby, Crosby Ravensworth, Asby, Brougham, Isel and Kirklinton.

In 1597 there was evidence of recusants in Crosthwaite, Sebergham, Wetheral, Warwick, Patterdale (Barton parish), Askham, Warcop, Dufton, Appleby, Crosby Ravensworth, Morland and Brough-under-Stainmore in the Carlisle Diocese, so they were spread throughout the area.

The impression given is of a church fighting against considerable odds both in the religious and secular fields. Yet in spite of this and persistent episcopal complaints of laxity and poor quality the Church continued to expand, particularly in Westmorland and the area north of the Sands in the diocese of Chester.

Parochial rights were given to the chapels at Crosthwaite (1556), Troutbeck (1562), Hawkshead (1578), Killington and Firbank (1583), Coniston (1586), Windermere (1587). Chapels were established at Langdale (1571), Long Sleddale (1571), Blawith (1577), Egton cum Newland (1577), Satterthwaite (1577), Ulpha (1577), Walney (1577), Colton (1578), and Witherslack (1581).

Why this expansion under what would appear to be unfavourable conditions when there was little evidence of religious fervour? The answer probably lies in the geographical or social field. At last the border ingredient of the area was of less significance, with peace between the two countries. Thus there was greater security with the resultant increase in population and with this a development in agriculture and in industry, particularly in the south where the environment was less harsh and where communications with other parts of the country were shorter and easier.

So at the start of the seventeenth century the religious and secular situations in Cumbria were somewhat confusing. As has already been said Bishop Robinson was reporting to Secretary Cecil that in his diocese the clergy were for the most part "utterly unlearned, unable to read English truly, were in some cases careless and idle where congregations were often without fear of God, and distinctly adulterers, thieves and murderers. Many chapels were unserviced and some of the border churches were 'walls without coverings'."

Again in 1617 Bishop Snowden writes "The citie of Carlisle is in great ruins and extreme poverty. In the country at large many of the meaner sort live dispersedly in cottages, or little farms scarcely sufficient for their necessary maintenance, whereby idleness, thefts and robberies are occasioned. The state ecclesiastique is highly weakened not only by Impropriations served by poor vicars and multitudes of base hirelings, but by compositions contracted in the troubled times and now prescribed yet there are some show of grave and learned pastors."

With the Scottish-English Union, Carlisle ceased to be of much importance.

Bishop Snowden in 1617 writes "citizens (of Carlisle) exercised no arts or trades and had no other means of livelihood except fishing". In fact Carlisle became a small market town, more inward looking and less worthy of consideration by the Crown. This was the temporary lull in its turbulent history before further upheavals during the period of the Commonwealth. Three officers on holiday visiting Carlisle in 1634 wrote "The Cathedral was nothing so fair and stately as those they had seen, but more like a great wild country church; as it appeared outwardly so it was inwardly neither beautiful not adorned one whit . . . . The communion also was administered and received in a wild and irreverent manner." Certainly Cumberland and Westmorland according to tax assessments at this time were the two poorest counties in England. Yet in spite of all this the church continued to expand, not yet in terms of new parishes, but by further chapels coming into use for the first time, by restoration or rebuilding: in the Carlisle Diocese – Swindale, Stainmore (1608), Arthuret (1609), Martindale, Kirk-andrews (1635); in Chester Diocese – Burneside (1602), Colton (1603), Ireleth (1608), Staveley-in-Cartmel (1618), Rampside (1621), Lindale (1627), Middleton (1635), Whitehaven (1642). More it will be noted in the south of the region.

It has been said that social life in the Middle Ages consisted of three main ingredients – war, agriculture, industry. By 1600 the first had largely disappeared, agriculture remained fairly constant and industry was beginning to develop. Here was the wind of change which will be discussed later. Suffice it here to note the development of mining for copper, silver and lead in the Newlands, Keswick area, particularly during the reign of Elizabeth I with the immigration of Germans, the working of coal at Distington (1614) with exports from Whitehaven (1650) and the wool trade centred on Kendal.

Presumably the church was still trying, not very successfully, to recover from the upheaval caused by the Dissolution of the Monasteries and the confiscation of much of the material wealth of the parishes and diocese while economically consolidation was taking place – a weakening of religious ties with a strengthening of economic ones.

CHAPTER 5

1640-1700 The Commonwealth and the start of Non-Conformity

And then in mid-century the whole fabric of the church was again subjected to revolutionary change – the puritan revolution and the consequent period of the Commonwealth 1643-1660 from which it never really recovered or perhaps more accurately it never completely regained its supremacy.

From the point of view of this account there is no need to go into the historical detail of this period which saw the temporary ending of episcopacy by 1643 along with the end of the Book of Common Prayer. Cumbria suffered greatly, for as a result of the civil war, by 1650 the Cathedral nave, chapter house, prebendal residences and part of the deanery and cloisters had been destroyed and the cathedral dignitaries ejected. Rose Castle, the house of the Bishop was burnt and the Chapter library was stolen. Part of the Deanery was used for 'manufacturing' purposes. Twenty-one clergy in the Carlisle diocese and ten in that of Chester (Coupland and Kendale) were ejected because of unwillingness to espouse the Presbyterian cause or for other reasons. Examples of ejections are found in a manuscript in Kendal Parish Church from the library of the Rev. John Crosby (1732) giving Minutes of the Committee "for ejecting of Scandalous Ignorant and Insufficient Ministers and Schoolmasters in the four northern counties at Penrith – Nov. 1655 to Feb. 1656".[1]

1. Offences against the late Mr. William Kempe of Windermere who is "Guilty of profanacon of ye Lord's Day, frequent quarreling and feightinge neglect of preachinge and prayinge on Lord's Day and is hereby declared and adjudged scandallous and to be ejected out of ye Rectory of Windermere. Penrith, Jan. 28th 1656.
2. Whereas Mr. ffrancis Bainbrigge of Troutbecke appeared before us this day according to Summons to give satisfaction of his ability and fitness for the work of the Ministry who upon his examination by ye Ministers in ye

[1] C. & W.A.A.S., n.s., xxiv, art. vii, *Ejected Ministers in Westmorland and Cumberland.*

Ordinance named whose names are subscribed appeared to be very Ignorant as by his answers to the questions propounded to him remaining in the hands of the Register to this Committee appears it is therefore ordered declared and adjudged that the said Mr. ffrancis Bainbrigge is Ignorant and altogether unfit for the worke of the Ministry and fit to be ejected ... and order him to departe out of the parish with his family and goods. Penrith, Jan. 30th 1656.

But more important because more permanent was the opportunity for the rise of different sects, Independents and Presbyterians. In 1652, George Fox first preached in the area at Firbank in Westmorland and so founded the Society of Friends (see p. 78). By 1653 there were the makings of Presbyterian associations (but not of Presbyterian government with elders, classes, synods, etc.) linking with Independents, examples being, Greystoke, Penrith, Edenhall, Skelton, Hutton, Addington – near the main north-south communication lines. In fact between 1643 and 1660 the principal churches of the Carlisle diocese were serviced either by resident or itinerant ministers of the Presbyterian, Independent or Baptist persuasion, the first-named predominating.

Yet when the episcopacy was restored in 1660 at the Restoration there is no evidence of parish disintegration in spite of the fact that the diocese was in a desperate situation. In fact by 1662 when with the Act of Uniformity (1659) and revision of the prayer book there was much evidence that rehabilitation was already begun. By 1662 for instance 22 of the dispossessed clergy were reinstated, the other 9 refusing to accept the Book of Common Prayer. Chapelries continued to be rebuilt or built:[2]

Carlisle Diocese: St. Ninian and St. Wilfred, Brougham (1658-60), Mallerstang (1663), Soulby (1663), Lowther Hall Chapel (1666), Armathwaite (1668), Roughton Head (1678), Nichol Forest (1678), Wreay (1679), Thursby (1681), High Head or Ivegill (1682), Camerton (1694).

Chester Diocese: Seathwaite (1650), Satterthwaite (1675), Firbank (1691), St. Nicholas, Whitehaven (1693), Old Hutton (1699).

It is difficult to assess the effect of the political and religious upheaval on the ordinary inhabitants and one suspects that it was less than is generally supposed. In 1660 there were still few roads and no public conveyances. Trade and commerce were only beginning to develop so

[2] *Carlisle Episcopal Register.*

the geography of the region must have still brought about a static and inward looking population. The main route of the region was still the north-south one from the border through Carlisle to Penrith, Kendal and Lancaster via the Eden and Lune valleys and the Presbyterian influence was most apparent on this line. It is estimated that between 1st August, 1662 and 1st August, 1663, 26,440 head of cattle passed through Cumberland on their way south to English markets.[3]

But it will be noticed that the rehabilitation of the Church of England was within the existing framework of parishes so one can assume that either there was no significant increase in the population or that with increasing population the number of adherents to the Church remained reasonably constant. The latter seems to be the more likely in view of the increasing divergence in religious views seen through the emergence of different sects. "In no domain did the Restoration mark so profoundly vital a change in the national life as it did in the religious domain ... the settlement imposed by the Uniformity Act (1662) definitely closed the doors of the national church to the non-conformists Presbyterians, and Independents alike. From 1662 the history of the Church of England no longer covers the whole of the ground becoming the story of merely such portions of the community as elect to be of its membership; and such as do not so elect occupying each their own ground and have each their separate history. What has hitherto been a single thread of history is divided henceforth into strands each leading far asunder."[4]

Throughout the seventeenth century and in fact from the time of the Dissolution of the Monasteries and the break with Rome, Roman Catholicism was practiced in Cumbria secretly and furtively. Foreign-bred emissaries mainly from Douai in France set up secret missions led by John Bost, as early as 1580. By the end of the century it is reckoned that there were over 20 priests actively engaged with the greatest following in Westmorland and in the Chester Diocese (see p. 71).

"Its (R.C.) history during the remainder of the seventeenth century and throughout the whole of the eighteenth and part of the nineteenth century is the history of a mission church lurking in secret with more or less toleration and persecution according to the fluctuating spirit of the time."[4]

[3] N. Nicholson, *Cumberland and Westmorland* (Robert Hale, London, 1949).
[4] *V.C.H.*, *Lancashire*, vol. 2 (University of London, reprint 1966).

During the seventeenth century the recusants were sustained by a number of well-known families, including the Stricklands of Sizergh, Flemings of Rydal, Ducketts of Grayrigg and the Howards of Naworth, but on the whole numbers did not increase much with probably about 500 actively concerned. In 1687, 138 persons were confirmed at Witherslack by Bishop John Leyburne, Vicar Apostolic of England. Note again the distribution. It is concerned with two of the main Cumbrian communication routes – north-south Carlisle-Penrith-Kendal-Lancaster and east-west Carlisle-Penrith-Stainmore-Yorkshire. This recalls the days of the Anglian 'invasion' of Cumbria in the seventh and eighth centuries (see p. 20).

But it was not the Roman Catholics who threatened the strength of the Church of England; it was the dissenters, non-conformists and above all in the last quarter of the seventeenth century the Quakers or Society of Friends.

It was in 1652 that George Fox entered Cumbria after his vision on Pendle Hill and met a group of people at Sedbergh (Briggflatts) who called themselves 'seekers', people who were not happy in Anglican liturgy nor in the theology of the dissenters. He then preached at Firbank in Westmorland and during that year made his headquarters at Swarthmoor near Ulverston in the house of Judge Fell. His itineraries for 1652 included Lancaster (where he was arrested for 'blasphemy', but was acquitted), Aldingham, Rampside, Dalton, Isle of Walney, Baycliffe and Gleaston. Thus he quickly gained adherents in Cartmel and Furness. His first contacts were in South Westmorland (Lonsdale, Chester Diocese) where at Preston Patrick he met a further group of 'seekers', who met monthly. They were led by a man called Thomas Taylor and came from a wide area of South Westmorland – Sedbergh, Yealand, Kellet, Kendal, Underbarrow, Crosthwaite, Grayrigg and Hutton. And so Preston Patrick became known as the 'Galilee of Quakerism', for Fox took over the leadership of this group and very quickly became a dominant figure in the religious life of South Cumbria. He travelled as far north as Carlisle where again he was arrested temporarily, but in 1653 his itinerary included Bootle, Cockermouth, Brigham, Caldbeck, Carlisle, Wigton. By 1657 meetings were being held in Westmorland at Strickland Head (for the Strickland, Penrith, Shap areas), at Newby Stones, Grayrigg, Ravenstonedale, Hutton and Kendal, the last named becoming a very influential centre.

It is interesting to note that this distribution is not unlike that of the very early pre-Norman Church with a concentration on the periphery of the Lake District, and by anticipating the eighteenth century this peripheral character was strengthened for in 1750 it was reported that in Cumberland there were nine parishes with 10 or more Quaker families, at Bromfield, Burgh-by-Sands (28 families), Caldbeck (29 families), Holm Cultram (30 families), Greystoke, Kirklinton (32 families), Stanwix, Stapleton, Wigton (58 families).[5]

Many of the Quaker meetings were in private houses, but quite soon special meeting houses were being erected and burial grounds established. In South Westmorland, Furness and Cartmel nine such houses were established by the early eighteenth century at Colthouse (Hawkshead), Rook How (Rusland), Swarthmoor, Height (Cartmel Fell), Misslet (between Bowness and Staveley), Kendal, Preston Patrick and Grayrigg (see Map 17). At Colthouse a burial ground was

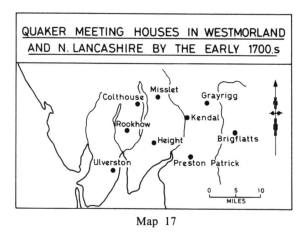

Map 17

established as early as 1659 (and incidentally is still in use in 1980). In the northern part of Cumbria, houses were established at Pardshaw (1677) and in Carlisle (1702).

Quakers were certainly a dedicated people, some would call them aggressive, for they fell foul of the established church. In 1660 "the

[5] C. M. L. Bouch & G. P. Jones, *The Lake District Counties 1500-1800* (Manchester University, 1961).

Quakers were the only people who ostentatiously defied the new enactments".[6]

In reports on conventicles (i.e. non-Anglican religious meetings of five or more persons) in 1669 it was reported that at Height "a place on the moors, there useth to be a great assembly of Quakers above 1000".[7] At a time when the learned professions were barred to them – they were forbidden the Universities until 1696 (Act of Affirmation) – they quickly established themselves as leaders of industry and trade. Thomas Rawlinson of Graythwaite, a friend of George Fox, became the leading ironmaster in the Furness area, and his family, along with the Fords, Crossfields and Backhouses came to own no less than 10 furnaces and 10 forges. The Backbarrow Iron Works flourished during the eighteenth century, when full advantage was taken of ample supplies of coppice timber for charcoal burning and the many streams provided power for working the bellows for the bloomeries. Pony trains carried the iron and its products to the Midlands and south-west where contacts were made with other Quakers. Quakers were also involved in mining. Edward Wright for instance founded the Quaker Lead Co. in the 1790s with mines in the Alston area and round Skiddaw near Keswick and Caldbeck, another reminder of the importance of the geological structures in Cumbria. In Kendal the names of Roger Wakefield and Richard Crewdson are associated with the traditional textile industry.

What of the other religious groups outside the established church? The advent of the 'dissenters' or non-conformists was less dramatic and development was slower than that of the Quakers, but perhaps more durable. It is more a story of the eighteenth and nineteenth centuries. It was in the south of Cumbria that non-conformity began, the earliest reference being to the chapel at Tottlebank in 1669 of the Congregational persuasion. Its first minister was the ejected vicar of Staveley-in-Cartmel, Camelford by name. It was soon to become a Baptist chapel (listed in 1773) along with a congregation at Hawkshead. In 1669 also there was evidence of 'anabaptists' at Cartmel.[8] Such congregations were legalised by the 'Declaration of Indulgence' in

---

[6] V.C.H., Lancashire, vol. 2.

[7] For further information see William Braithwaite, The Beginnings of Quakerism, 2nd edn., Henry J. Cadbury, ed. (Cambridge Univ., 1961).

[8] V.C.H., Lancashire, vol. 2.

1671 by King Charles II and by Act of Toleration in 1689. By the end of the century there were chapels at Crook (near Windermere), Cockermouth and Heversham (at Stainton), and in the Kendal area where six licences for ministers were issued after 1671 (there was one other in Westmorland at Heversham). The activity was taking place in the Chester Diocese, but Carlisle did not escape. By 1669 there were meetings of 'Independents' at Bridekirk, Brampton, Hesket and Lazonby, with Presbyterians at Penrith and Ravenstonedale where churches existed. These were small scattered communities, with a distribution reflecting personal reactions to the church on the part of individuals rather than any environmental influences.

Richard Frankland, an ejected minister from Auckland, Durham, who was a Yorkshireman of Rathmel founded an academy there for dissenters in 1669 and shortly afterwards moved to Natland near Kendal. He was driven from there because he contravened the Oxford Act (1665) or Five Mile Act, whereby no ejected minister could reside within 5 miles of a parish church, but he later returned to the area and was successful at Dawson Fold, Crosthwaite and Hartbarrow at Cartmel Fell before finally moving out of the area to Sheffield in 1686.[9] This illustrates the difficulties for those wishing to develop nonconformity at this time. It would appear that pressure for such sects not of the Church of England came from outside rather than in. George Fox was not a Cumbrian and he first saw the 'light' in Lancashire; the Baptist movement also came from Lancashire, established by the Rossendale Church,[10] again probably a distribution representing the reactions of individuals.

So the seventeenth century ended with the Church of England no longer all embracing. The religious influence of the parish church was declining and its secular nature increasing in importance. After the Union of Scotland and England had taken place the importance of Carlisle decreased and it became a small market town. No longer were the Bishops expected to be diplomats, soldiers and courtiers and theoretically at any rate could concentrate on their religious duties. The parish is recognised as a territorial division and the church a civil centre for the local community with rents and tithes paid there. Here too land

[9] F. Nicholson & E. Axon, *The Older Non-conformity in Kendal* (Titus Wilson, Kendal).

[10] *V.C.H.*, *Lancashire*, vol. 2.

was sold and conveyed. This century saw a very important development in landholding. The number of freehold farms increased with the rise of the 'Statesmen', well to do farmers, living on the land that they owned and working it themselves. Here again was evidence of the decline of the influence of the church as the custodian of the land of the parish although it still retained its importance as the domestic, social, recreational and cultural centre.

CHAPTER 6

1700-1850 The Impact of the Agricultural and Industrial Revolutions on Religious Observance – The Age of Wesley

G. M. Trevelyan[1] sums up the period 1700-1850 in England from the religious point of view as follows:

> After the Restoration, the members of the landowning class who attended conventicles and suffered persecution as nonconformists were a mere handful. Anglicanism became distinctively the upper-class religion far more completely than it had been in the days of Elizabeth or Laud. There were indeed still a certain number of Roman Catholic country gentlemen, especially in Lancashire and Northumberland; they were shut out from all participation in local and national government by laws which the King was however, occasionally able to break for their benefit. Otherwise the upper class, the gentlemen of England, were socially united by common conformity to the Anglican worship. Henceforth the services of the parish church were under the special patronage of the ladies and gentlemen in the family pews; the great body of the congregation were their dependents, the farmers and labourers of the village.
>
> The dissenting congregations on the other hand alike in time of persecution and toleration were made up of men who prided themselves on their independence, and who liked to feel that the chapel and its minister belonged to themselves.
>
> Thus the social character of English religious divisions was stereotyped at the Restoration and continued with little change until the Victorian era.

Anglicans, Dissenters, Roman Catholics; these three groups of people and particularly the first two, with their differences in religious loyalties and observances set the pattern for Christianity in this country, one of division rather than unity, throughout the eighteenth and nineteenth centuries. As has been seen this divisiveness had been developing in the later years of the previous century so it was a continuing process. In addition the set-up tended to sharpen class distinction for reasons stated, distinctions which became more marked as time went on because of the way that economic life developed in

---

[1] G. M. Trevelyan, *English Social History* (Longmans Green, 1948).

England. From now on social and economic conditions have great bearing on the pattern of religious life and both are basically geographical.

So before any further consideration of church and chapel organisation it is necessary to say something of the social and economic background.

The eighteenth and nineteenth centuries saw two great (fortunately comparatively peaceful) revolutions – those of agriculture and industry respectively, marking great changes in the way of life of many people and great changes in their attitude to life, which was bound to have repercussions in religious life.

The Agrarian Revolution began in the late seventeenth century, but it was in the eighteenth century that it made its greatest impact in Great Britain, causing profound changes in farming types, techniques and land tenure. First came Jethro Tull's horse-hoeing husbandry with the sowing of seeds in drills, resulting in a relative saving in the amount of seed used and an increase in yield because of greater freedom of the land from weeds. Then came the introduction and experimentation by people like Coke of Holkham and 'Turnip' Townsend, of new crops – turnips. potatoes and temporary grasses. This resulted in changes in field cultivation with new rotations with the elimination of fallow and also a greater regional diversity in the types of grain which could be successfully grown. Thirdly came changes in the quality and type of stock kept, as exemplified in the work of Robert Bakewell of Dishley in Leicestershire, held to be the founder of modern stock breeding. Medieval farming had always been restricted by lack of winter feed for animals so that all, except breeding animals, had to be slaughtered in the autumn and the meat dried and cured for winter use. With the new rotations and introduction of grasses and turnips, this restriction no longer applied and with increased yields an increasing number of animals could be kept. Also in medieval times indiscriminate pasturing of stock on the common land kept quality low, but with changes in land tenure resulting in more and more field enclosures, selective breeding could take place.

All these changes had, as well, the effect of expanding commercial agriculture with greater interchange of agricultural products between the various regions within the country, and the necessary preliminaries for this were improvements in communications. It is not easy to be precise as to which was cause and which effect on these changes, but obviously natural conditions of relief, weather and relative isolation or otherwise of position in the country, resulted in differences between the various regions both in kind and scale of changes. It is not surprising to find that Cumbria's involvement in the 'new' agriculture was late in coming and somewhat limited in scope because of its geographical position in the north-west corner of England. This area has never been notable for arable farming and thus it did not easily fit in with the type of farming based on the Norfolk Four Course system, essentially arable and more suited to the lighter soils and drier eastern side of the country.

Before relating these changes to Cumbria and being more precise about them in assessing their impact on the church it might be more profitable to complete the geographical picture by considering the onset of the 'Industrial Revolution' still in its infancy in the eighteenth century and not fully effective until 100 years later i.e. after 1850.

Medieval England was in industrial terms, essentially a nation of craftsmen, and on the whole self-supporting. During that time, and largely through the resourcefulness of the monastic houses trade developed with other countries, particularly in wool and woollen cloth, but generally speaking the craftsman served his local community as blacksmith or farrier, weaver, wheelwright, etc. Wool was the staple fibre for cloth making and for knitting, coal was worked but its use was limited, metals were mined and worked on a relatively small scale, iron for farm implements, domestic utensils and 'engines' of war, lead for such things as church roofs and piping. There was gold and silver for coinage and precious objects, leather for footwear, saddles etc., and of course timber for building purposes from domestic utensils to carts and ships as well as for making charcoal used in smelting. Interchange of commodities took place in the various market towns conveniently spaced at nodal points in each region. But during the sixteenth and seventeenth centuries the local and regional markets were just beginning to give way to more national markets which stimulated demand. This necessitated larger industrial units and often a change in their location; to river valleys where water power was available to run the machines or, in the case of iron smelting to places where there was abundance of coppice timber for the making of charcoal.

The two vital industrial changes which were largely initiated in the eighteenth century and developed in the nineteenth were, first the introduction of machine industry as opposed to handicraft industry when the worker became a minder of machines which did the processing rather than a craftsman who processed the raw material himself, and second the machines were power driven, not by water which kept a dispersed and rural distribution but by steam power through coal which brought about a nucleated and urban distribution. Thirdly, new inventions produced new and bigger machines with new techniques resulting in greater production. World trade brought about ever greater and greater demands so that communications had to be improved. Here again invention resulted in the development of water borne traffic, the improvement of road surfaces associated with McAdam and Telford, the turnpikes, to be soon followed by the railways.

How then do the agricultural and industrial revolutions bear on the religious life of the people of Cumbria? It is not difficult to be precise about the changes so far as religious organisation and observance is concerned, but it is not possible to quantify the social implications. For many people the quality of life changed with resultant change in attitude to religion. For many, no longer was the parish church the focus of their activities, and the church was slow to realise this. Not so the dissenters.

But to deal first with the Anglican (Established) church. "The History and Antiquities of the Counties of Westmorland and Cumberland", written by Joseph Nicholson and Richard Burn, was published in London in 1777 and in it are listed the parishes in the Diocese of Carlisle and those in the Chester Diocese. Comparing this list with that of the parishes in 1291 (see p. 62) it is clear that for nearly 500 years parish changes were extremely limited. In the Carlisle Diocese the only new parishes were Kirkandrews-on-Esk, Carlisle St. Mary (formed from the former monastic house), Westward, Allhallows, Flimby (ex Camerton), Newton Reigny and Langwathby (ex Edenhall). In the Chester Diocese (former Archdeaconry of Richmond) they were Waybergthwaite, Drigg, Little Beckermet, Arlecdon, Colton and Hawkshead.

The records in the Diocesan Registry in Carlisle and the Archives Department of the Cumbria County Council show that between 1777 and 1850 the following new parishes were created; Carlisle (Holy Trinity), Houghton, Whitehaven (Holy Trinity), Whitehaven (St. James), Whitehaven (St. Nicholas), Whitehaven (Christchurch),

Thornthwaite, Holme (St. Cuthbert); in the Chester Diocese came Workington (St. John), Setmurphy, Wythop, Haverthwaite and Rusland.

Besides the paucity of change, the pattern of those changes is not unfamiliar (see Map 18); they are either in the lower reaches of the Eden valley or along the western and southern perimeter. The highland centre remains undisturbed.

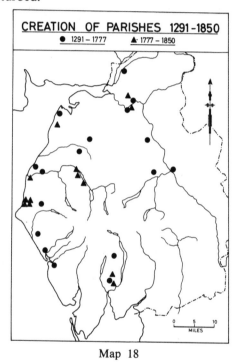

CREATION OF PARISHES 1291-1850
● 1291 – 1777   ▲ 1777 – 1850

0   5   10
MILES

Map 18

As has already been suggested (see p. 82) the strength of the Established Church lay in the support given to it by the landed gentry and the upper class generally, with their many dependents providing numerically the greater part of the congregation. During the eighteenth century it would appear that the changes in agricultural practices strengthened the landowners at the expense of the freeholders or 'statesmen', whose numbers declined during this period. Generally speaking the rich got richer and the poor poorer. With great improvements in agriculture one would have expected that all would have benefited but with the introduction of new crops and particularly the improvement in the quality of stock there came the necessity for additional capital in the case of the former and enclosures of land in the latter case. The enclosures of the common land and the fell slopes deprived many villagers of long held rights and made them more and more dependent on the landowners. Labour became ever cheaper. Incidentally, it is because of the abundance of labour that the Lake District owes miles of familiar stone walls dividing the valley fields and the upper slopes as they snake over the landscape. Many of the statesmen farmers could not afford the necessary equipment for the new husbandry and it is reckoned that their numbers halved between 1770 and 1820. Tenant farmers on the other hand benefited because they could usually rely on the capital of the owner. These dates (1770-1820) too are significant in explaining the static nature of church organisation in the earlier part of the eighteenth century. It is not the first time that attention has been drawn to the isolation of Cumbria so that ideas from the more southerly parts of England took time to penetrate. Thomas West in his 'Antiquities of Furness' was complaining that in 1773, "one general obstacle to improvement and advancement of agriculture in Furness is the mixed lands or township fields . . . domestic economy calls for the improvement of every acre; this can never be done where there is common pasture, by which every man has it in his power to prevent his neighbour's industry". Thus change came slowly with the introduction of temporary grasses, particularly clover, potatoes and turnips for winter feed only in the second half of the century (clover 1752, turnips 1754, wheat 1754). Oats and barley were still the staple crops at the end of the century, with wheat only being grown on the periphery of the area.

In Cumbria it was reported "wheat is a modern production here; a general opinion used to prevail that wheat could not be grown in many parts of this country". It was into the Carlisle Plain and the West Cumberland coastland that wheat had been introduced . . . and into Low Furness, but not into the higher lands towards the moors.[2]

The two areas mentioned indicate a climatic control; low relief and less rainfall, yet at the same time it may be that these areas were more open to changing attitudes with increasing independence – hence the

[2] W. Smith, *An Economic Geography of Great Britain* (Methuen, 1949).

desire for more separate parishes. The advances made by the end of the eighteenth century in the areas of low relief are illustrated by the clergy crop return of 1801 for the parish of Sebergham to the south of Carlisle. Of the 1,400 acres under cultivation (about 1/5th of the total acreage), 194 were of wheat while 680 were of oats. In addition there were 135 acres of barley, 88 of pease, 72 of turnips, 48 of potatoes, 2·5 of rye and 0·5 of beans. So while oats remained the staple crop, diversification was taking place.

But grass farming was the main form of land utilisation particularly in the more hilly areas. Traditionally the sheep were kept on the fells during the summer and then sent to the coastal lowland in the winter where herbage was available and where weather conditions were more kindly – a form of transhumance begun during monastic times. Cattle were also kept usually of the Longhorn variety, but there was still the problem of winter feed with the result that dairy farming was minimal. Farms became larger in size as new methods and practices were brought into use, so that rural life tended to be dominated by the landed gentry and the large freeholders. The existing parochial set-up was quite adequate to deal with the gradual changing circumstances and consequent fairly static population.

But the polarisation of the rural social regime, along with the industrial changes which will be dealt with later, had two big effects on the church; one human and one material.

The human effect was in the changing status of the clergy. Throughout the history of the Carlisle Diocese there were constant complaints about the poor quality of the clergy, about absentee rectors, and about neglect of the churches themselves. In 1760 of 93 benefices in that part of Cumbria in the Chester Diocese for instance, 80 were worth only £50 per annum or less and 56 worth only £10 or less, sums hardly likely to attract many or good people. The eighteenth century saw some alteration of the problem, but Carlisle remained one of the poorest diocese in the country. To quote Trevelyan again; "It (the Established Church in the eighteenth century) was a church renowned for scholarship, culture and freedom. But little pressure was exerted either by episcopal authority or by public opinion to compel the clergy to exert themselves more than they wished. A living was regarded like a seat in Parliament or a College Fellowship, as a piece of patronage awarded as a favour and enjoyed as a privilege. The social gulf between rich and poor clergy was still almost as wide as in medieval times. But the proportion of the well-to-do was greater, for they now included not only prelates and pluralists but a number of resident parish clergy of good family and connections, living in the parsonage and attending to its duties. The rise in the value of tithes and glebe farms with the improvements in agriculture helped this development."[3]

It is reckoned that in Queen Anne's time of 10,000 livings in England, 5,597 were valued at less than £50 per annum, whereas by 1800 only 400 were below £150.

As in the case of the laity the rich clergy tended to become richer, but the poor became relatively poorer, i.e. the curates and readers.

Two examples of social status with accompanying privileges or lack of them, show that Cumbria was no exception, George Fleming, fifth son of Sir Daniel Fleming of Rydal was persuaded by his father to accept ordination, much against his will apparently, for he wrote to his father of his "natural aversion to it". Nevertheless he was ordained by Bishop Smith in Rose Castle in 1694, Bishop Smith being a relative. Thereafter the career of the Rev. George Fleming was as follows: 1695 Vicar of Aspatria, 1701 Canon of Carlisle Cathedral, 1703 Vicar of Stanwix and Kirkland, 1705 Archdeacon of Carlisle and Rector of Great Salkeld, 1727 Dean of Carlisle, 1735 Bishop of Carlisle. On the other hand Robert Robson, son of a Sebergham yeoman was ordained in 1748 yet in spite of repeated attempts failed to get a benefice for 33 years.

Edward Jackson was appointed Vicar of Colton in 1762 remaining there until 1789, holding also the living of Ulverston between 1786 and 1789. Socially he was on equal terms with the local gentry and a friend of the Cavendishes of Holker. His hobbies were appropriately hunting, shooting and fishing and he was also interested in botany, yet the reader (i.e. unordained) at Wythburn was paid only £3 per annum along with a hempen sark, whittlegate (the right to board for a given number of days per annum in the homes of local people) and goosegate (the right to have geese on the fell side). At Newlands the reader worked as clogger, tailer and butter print maker to eke out a living.

Pluralism was common and the practice aggravated the problem of poverty among curates who deputised for the holder of the benefice. In

[3] G. M. Trevelyan, *English Social History* (Longmans Green, 1948).

1799 for instance in the Deanery of Westmorland examples of the position *vis a vis* absentee benefice holders and curates were:

Value of living	Curates' Stipend (usually+clothes and Whittlegate)
£280	£36
270	30
120	20
80	20
80	16
60	15

Generally speaking however the eighteenth century saw a greater period of stability in Cumbria than had been known in earlier centuries so far as the church was concerned, and while it clung to some of the less worthy practices of the medieval period it benefited from the patronage of the upper classes, and the parish church regained some of its importance as a social centre particularly in rural areas. It is not therefore surprising that there was a great surge in building and 'restoring' of churches and chapels. Between 1747 and 1850, 60 churches and chapels were either built or restored in the Carlisle Diocese, and 47 in the Chester Deaneries. Examples of new churches in the Carlisle Diocese are: 1763, Maryport; 1767, Plumpton; 1830, Christchurch, Carlisle; 1831 Holy Trinity, Carlisle. Restorations included 1749, Uldale; 1777, Threlkeld; 1792, Bewcastle; 1832, Askham; 1846, St. Johns-in-the-Vale. In the Chester Diocese, examples are: new churches, 1753, St. James, Whitehaven; 1755, St. George's, Kendal; 1823, St. John's, Workington.

But the story so far is over-simplified and other factors must be taken into consideration. Parish formation is generally related to the distribution and size of population. The eighteenth century saw changes in population in Cumbria in a number of ways. Figures until the era of censuses beginning in 1801 are somewhat suspect, but in the late eighteenth and early nineteenth centuries a reasonably accurate picture can be obtained. Two sets of statistics are particularly relevant.

1. Total Population	1688 (Denton Survey)	1801	1831
Cumberland	60,000	117,230	169,681
Westmorland	27,000	40,805	55,041
Furness and Cartmel	n/a	17,887	24,311

2. *Urban population*

	1688	*1801*	*1831*	*1851*
Carlisle	5,060	10,221	20,000	26,310
Workington	945	5,716	6,415	6,280
Penrith	1,350	3,801	6,059	7,387
Whitehaven	1,110	11,300	17,000	14,190

By 1811 there were 12 towns in Cumberland each with more than 1,000 inhabitants constituting 40% of the total population, but there was a decline in numbers in 36 rural parishes with a decline too, in Westmorland between 1688 and 1801. For example Warcop was down by 3·8%, Ravenstonedale by 9%. In Westmorland too 29% of the population lived in four towns, viz. Kendal, Appleby, Kirkby Stephen and Kirkby Lonsdale. In 1811 in Cumberland 51,000 people depended on agriculture for a living, less than 50%, while 53,000 depended on industry and trade.

From the above figures it can be deduced that during this period the total population increased, but this increase was not evenly spread throughout the region. The agricultural rural areas tended to decrease while the urban centres increased. These urban centres were of two kinds; the market towns, most of considerable antiquity, and the new industrial ones, epitomised perhaps by Penrith and Whitehaven respectively. This change in population distribution obviously affected individual parishes, so that generally speaking the centre, north, and east of Cumbria saw little change, while the west and south saw the creation of what new parishes there were as seen, for instance in Whitehaven with four creations. Cumbria was essentially a rural area and as has already been said the changes in agriculture resulted in an increasing number of enclosures and a reduction in the number of farm units giving a surplus of labour. The drift to the towns had begun, but the church was not yet fully aware of its significance, a drift consequent on the inception of industry rather than the result of agricultural redundancy, although this latter was important.

But before dealing with the influence of industry which is now to become of increasing importance and significance to the church in Cumbria and throughout the whole of the country, there is one other linking topic. Commercial agriculture, industry and trade, the interchange of goods and people can only develop if means of communication are reasonably easy. Traditionally communications in Cumbria have not been easy due to the nature of the terrain and the distance from large markets. Writing about the early seventeen hundreds Moorman says "Distances were so great, roads so dangerous, means of travel so slow and English weather so treacherous that with the best will in the world a bishop could hardly see much of his clergy or even know who they were, moreover the difference in class between prelates and poor parish priest was so great that they could have had little in common".[4]

John Ogilby's road map of 1675 showed the major routes in Cumbria to be

(a) Kendal-Shap-Penrith-Carlisle,
(b) Egremont-Whitehaven-Workington-Cockermouth-Carlisle,
(c) Kendal-Ambleside-Keswick-Cockermouth,
(d) Newcastle-on-Tyne-Corby-Castle Carrock-Carlisle,
(e) Boroughbridge-Barnard Castle-Stainmore-Brough-Penrith.

These were in fact similar to the routes of the Roman roads still in use after 1400 years and with the advent of postal services and coaches these roads provided the main means of movement. It was during the eighteenth century that road improvements were taking place and were essential if communications were to keep pace with the economic changes. Thus the era of turnpikes began, to be continued well into the nineteenth century. By 1735 there was a thrice weekly postal service from Lancaster to Carlisle via Kendal and Penrith, this being increased to 6 times weekly in 1764. In 1781 there was a diligence between Preston and Carlisle by the same route completing the journey in a day, with connections to Glasgow and Edinburgh. By 1783 there were coaches from Manchester to Glasgow and Edinburgh and from Manchester to Ulverston and Whitehaven via the coastal route, while by 1825 routes added to the above covered Lancaster to Newcastle via Kirkby Stephen and Barnard Castle, and Lancaster to Whitehaven via Kendal, Keswick and Cockermouth. Note how certain places stand out as focal points. Carlisle, Kendal, Penrith. In addition there were wagons serving local routes distributing and collecting goods for the small ports, for instance of Ulverston, Whitehaven, Workington and Carlisle itself. The pack horse routes used in monastic days were still important particularly for the central mountainous areas. But generally speaking until the early nineteenth century with the advent of the Lake Poets and

[4] J. R. H. Moorman, *A History of the Church in England* (Adam & Charles Black, 1967).

the romantic period in literature the central core of Cumbria remained relatively unknown.

Taken by and large, in the eighteenth century the pattern of roads and bridle paths represented the status quo, but the beginning of public transport gave the opportunity for greater ease of movement which was becoming increasingly necessary with the economic expansion of the country at home and abroad. Hence the development of the market towns which were on important routes and the consolidation of parish units which with increasing population could only in time lead to an increase in their number.

While agricultural changes affected the life and organisation of the Established Church to some extent the consequences of industrial development were more far reaching. During the eighteenth and early nineteenth centuries changes in the type and scale of industry resulted in large urban centres and changes in population distribution. The first consequences of all this was greater diversity in religious allegiance and observance.

By 1800 almost all the iron produced in England by means of charcoal burning came from the Furness and Cartmel areas in the south of the region. Burnings were taking place in eight places. Backbarrow (1711), Cunsey (1711), Nibthwaite (1735), Duddon Bridge (1730), Newlands (Ulverston) (1746), Low Wood (Haverthwaite) (1748), Penny Bridge (1745), Wilson House, Lindale (1740). Here there was coppice timber available in quantity, although the large amounts required in the making of charcoal meant that sources had to be found as far away as Borrowdale and Troutbeck. The main haematite 'ore pits' or mines were in the Dalton area, at Whitriggs, Lindal Moor, Lindal Cote and Crossgates. Other mines were at Stainton and Adgarley.

Between one-third and a half of the ore mined was used locally and the rest exported. Much was sent from Ulverston by ship to South Wales, much helped after the construction of the Ulverston Canal in 1796, and in 1807 11,202 tons of ore were shipped along with 682 tons of pig iron. At this time too eyes were being directed to the channel between the mainland and Walney Island with the small port of Piel which was also being used to export iron ore on a small scale from 1782 onward. By 1790 a new larger jetty was constructed and by 1842 three further jetties had been built, largely to deal with the iron ore trade.

Thus Barrow-in-Furness, a hamlet in the parish of Dalton began its meteoric rise which belongs to the post-1850 era.

While during the eighteenth century the use of charcoal as the fuel for furnaces and forges persisted in South Cumbria (then North Lancashire) great technological changes were taking place elsewhere with the onset of the Industrial Revolution. So far as the iron industry was concerned it was Quaker families who played the major role. As early as 1709 the first Abraham Darby was experimenting at Coalbrookdale with iron smelting using coal (coked) as the heating element and his methods were widely adopted as the century progressed, at first jealously guarded by the Quaker iron-masters who formed family groups. Such groups were the Lloyds of Wales and Birmingham, the Darby-Reynolds of Coalbrookdale, the Fownes, Cotton, Milnes, etc. of Yorkshire. These families spread their influence widely for in addition to their industrial activities, many felt it their duty to travel and speak on behalf of the Quaker movement or Society of Friends as it came to be known, attending yearly and other meetings "mingling in a unified whole their activities as Quakers with the concerns of a large and intricate combine of ironmasters".[5]

The Fell-Rawlinson group in Furness were no exception and must have come into contact with and be aware of the new coking methods. Two of the most important entrepeneurs in the iron industry at this time were Nehemiah Champion of Bristol and Samuel Milner of Bewdley. The Rawlinson's sent pig iron to both as is evidenced by their journal and account book of 1713[6] and in return received such items as iron pots, kettles, Carolina tar, oil and cider, these distributed by Rawlinson's pack animals to markets in Kendal, Penrith, Hawkshead and Lancaster. It is known that the iron pots and kettles were acquired by Champion from Coalbrookdale. Some of this trade was carried on by means of pack horse trains and some by sea. Just as Thomas Rawlinson travelled as far south as Devonshire so others moved north on behalf of the Society. One such was John Kelsall who was associated with the Darby group at Dolgyn near Dolgellau and at Dolobran in Merioneth during the first half of the century. So ideas are disseminated.

It was perhaps the abundance of local coppice timber for charcoal

[5] A. Raistrick, *Quakers in Science and Industry* (David & Charles, 1968).
[6] *Rawlinson Journal and Account Book*, f. 321.

burning which delayed the use of coking coal in Furness and West Cumberland until well after 1750. But the number of people employed was relatively small and could be contained in existing urban and rural areas so that on the whole existing parishes could serve them adequately. But note the new parishes of Haverthwaite and Rusland (see p. 86). Also by 1800 the mining of haematite iron ore was taking place further north in West Cumberland, at first for export via the sea to Scotland, but post-1750 also for smelting near the mines using local coal, although it was difficult to make coke from it. The use of coke, in plentiful supply, meant that larger amounts of iron could be produced.

Furnaces were set up at Little Clifton (1750), Frizington (1750), Seaton (1762) and Maryport (1784). At the same time, and partly because of, the coal measures of the Carboniferous period were being exploited, particularly after 1750 when Newcomen's engine for pumping water out of mine workings was introduced; 4 engines by 1777 and 8 by 1790. The mines were at Whitehaven, Workington and Distington. The proximity of coal and iron ore in West Cumberland resulted in the area having the greatest population increases (see p. 90) and therefore the bulk of the new parishes (see p. 85).

But the main effect of industrial development at this stage was to strengthen non-conformity, not the Established Church. As Trevelyan said (see p. 82) the dissenting congregations were made up of men who prided themselves on their independence, and it was they, by and large, who were the innovators, who established and developed the machine industries, the great exception being the Lowther family, the biggest landowners in the region. The new workers in industry owed no allegiance to the landowning class and therefore, unlike the rural population were not bound to the established church.

Something has already been said about the Quakers, the Society of Friends who made their greatest impact in South Cumbria in the Furness, Cartmel and Kendal areas. It was during the second half of the eighteenth century that the seeds were sown for another and greater movement in non-conformity.

Between 1748 and 1790 John Wesley visited the region twenty-six times, during his many tours through the British Isles and America.

Trevelyan has this to say "In the early years of George III . . . in the new industrial and mining districts (of England) the neglected inhabitants altogether escaped the ministrations of the Establishment, whose antiquated geography was seldom brought up to date by the creation of new parishes. That mission field was left to Wesley."

It must be remembered that Wesley himself was missioning from within the Established Church of which he was an ordained member, and it was only after his death that the movement he started seceded, taking nearly 50 years in the process. In the meantime however he was forming societies and organising them into circuits. By 1766 there were 25 such circuits in England, including one in Lancashire. To quote Trevelyan[7] again, "The greatest and most justly famous of the manifestations of Methodism was the revivalist preaching of the Wesleys and Whitefield which deeply moved a vast mass of human beings hitherto neglected by church and state.... By forming his converts into permanent congregations he began a new chapter in the religious, social and educational history of the working class. The coincidence in time of Wesley and the Industrial Revolution had profound effects upon England for generations to come."

During the forty years of John Wesley's association with Cumbria he ranged far and wide, but not with equal intensity. According to his journal the places in Cumberland which he visited (with the number of visits in brackets after each) were: Whitehaven (26), Cockermouth (19), Carlisle (12), Solway Firth (7) en route to or from Scotland, Keswick (5), Wigton (4), Penrith (3), Lorton (3), Gamblesby (3), twice each to Branthwaite, Clifton, Gins (Whitehaven), Longtown, Nenthead, and once each to Bootle, Bowness, Alston, Alston Moor, Ballantyn, Caldbeck, Drigg, Hartside, Hensingham, Houghton, Millom, Muncaster, Penruddock, Ravenglass, Seaton, Skinburness, Workington.[8] Their distribution is more clearly seen in Map 19 where they are quantified.

More detailed analysis of the Journal itself[9] shows that he first visited Cumbria in September 1749 staying for two weeks with a brief detour to the Alston area and Hinely Hill where he often stayed the night when travelling. Much of the time he was based on Whitehaven (with Gins and Hensingham) and commented, "The work in Whitehaven resembles that in Athlone more than it does any other which I have seen in England. It runs with a swift and wide stream; but it does not go deep.

[7] G. M. Trevelyan, *English Social History* (Longmans Green, 1948).

[8] C. & W.A.A.S., n.s., xlvii, T. H. Bainbridge, 'John Wesley's Travels in Cumberland'.

[9] Rev. John Wesley, *The Works of*, vols. I to IV (London, 1829).

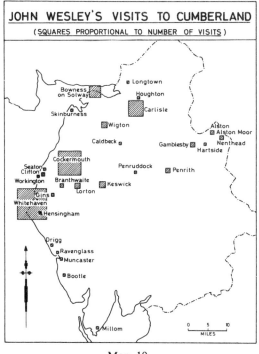

Map 19

A considerable part of the town seems moved, but extremely few are awake; and scarce three have found a sense of the pardoning love of God."

Between then and his last visit in May 1788, at the age of 85, when in Whitehaven "the congregation rejoiced much as they had not seen me for four years", he spent an average of one week every two years in Cumbria, always between April and September, a reminder of problems of travel in winter through upland areas where the weather was often inclement. Frequently he mentions heavy rain while travelling and when conditions prevented him from speaking out of doors. Nor was he impressed with some of the roads: "a great part of the road was miserably bad", he wrote of the journey from Cockermouth to Carlisle, and in the Gamblesby-Hartside area he rode "through miserable roads". Yet it would seem that he was conversant with the Ogilby road map (see p. 92) for most of his routes coincided with it. Map 20 illustrates four of his journeys in 1749, 1759, 1784 and 1786 respectively. He was particularly impressed with the mountains, getting lost on more than one occasion when weather conditions were bad and the mist was low. For instance, while travelling between Kendal and Whitehaven he wrote, "We were soon lost on the mountains .... A poor man piloted us over the next mountain the like of which I never beheld in Wales or Germany". Could this have been Whinlatter?

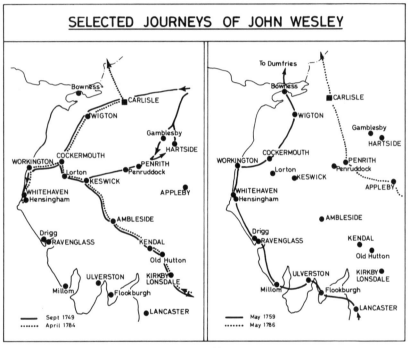

SELECTED JOURNEYS OF JOHN WESLEY

Map 20

Until 1772 Wesley travelled on horseback, but after that by chaise. On only one occasion did he use the coastal route, in May 1759 (see Map 20) from Lancaster via Flookburgh, Millom, Bootle and Ravenglass to Whitehaven, for ingress into the region from the south and his comments on the journey explain why. "But I have taken leave of the sand road", he wrote, "I believe it is ten measured miles shorter than the other (via Kendal, Ambleside, Keswick, Lorton, Cockermouth and Whitehaven), but there are four sands to pass so far from each other that it is scarcely possible to pass them all in one day, especially as you have all the way to do with a generation of liars who detain all travellers as long as they can, for their own gain as their neighbours. I can advise no stranger to go this way."

Wesley appears to have been something of a geographer as well as an evangelist. While in Whitehaven he wrote in his journal; "In travelling through Berkshire, Oxfordshire, Lancashire, Yorkshire, Westmorland and Cumberland, I diligently made two enquiries: the first, was concerning the increase or decrease of the people; the second concerning the increase or decrease of trade. As to the latter, it is, within these last two years, amazingly increased; in several branches in such a manner as has not been known in the memory of man. Such is the fruit of the entire civil and religious liberty which England now enjoys."

By 1773 a 'society' had been established in Cumberland, meeting in private houses and keeping alive the precept and tenets of the faith given during his preaching tours. These were based on self discipline, active evangelism and above all active philanthropy, as opposed to the 'latitudinarian' doctrine of the Church of tolerance and reasonableness in interpreting Christian doctrines. Bouch and Jones[10] write, "It (Methodism) was at once Puritan and Middle Class in character . . . . The citadel of this way of life was the middle class home, with its family worship, whence it went out to convert the souls, educate the minds and care for the bodies of the neglected poor."

The important thing of course, is that he concentrated his activity in West Cumberland with Whitehaven as the focal point. This is not surprising for here and in the immediate hinterland were the workers in industry – particularly the mining community and the professional classes associated with the new industrial undertakings (see p. 95). They were people owing allegiance neither to the Puritans of the early non-conformity nor to the Established Church, who might therefore be expected to be sympathetic to his crusade; those who had moved out of the paternalistic and autocratic regime of medieval England into the realities, and often harsh ones, of the industrial era. It is significant that he was particularly successful in Cornwall among the tin mining community, some of whom later migrated to Cumbria as iron and coal

---

[10] C. M. L. Bouch & G. P. Jones, *The Lake Counties 1500-1830 – A Social and Economic History* (Manchester, 1961).

mining developed bringing Methodism with them, and in the mining areas of the Pennines.

"John Wesley gave to the poor labourer, the outcast and even the criminal (reformed), alongside the thriving tradesman and the intellectuals, a place to fill and a job to do. For poverty and pain he offered the consolation of present ecstasy and the promise of future peace and salvation."[11]

He also used Whitehaven on a number of occasions as the port from which he sailed to the Isle of Man.

Yet for some reason he was not very successful in this north-western outpost and although in 1751 he claimed that 240 people attended his meeting in Whitehaven the numbers fluctuated and there were times when he evoked little response. In May 1752 while visiting Ulverston on his way south from Whitehaven to Kendal and Lancashire, he wrote, "Here a very convenient place for preaching was offered. But few people had any desire to hear. So I went quietly back to my inn." In April 1753 on arriving in Whitehaven he found that "the love of many was waxed cold", and in April 1770 at Cockermouth, "It was here a day of small things; the society consisting but of fifteen members". His main efforts were made elsewhere in the country.

It was after John Wesley's death in 1791 that the influence of Methodism was increasingly felt in Cumbria and in Cumberland rather than further south in Westmorland and North Lancashire. In Cumberland apart from the Alston area there were three chapels built before 1800: at Carlisle 1786, Wigton 1788, and the earliest at Workington in 1767, although congregations also existed at Penrith, Whitehaven and Wigton. By 1840, 23 more were built with another 14 by 1850. Thus by the middle of the nineteenth century 40 Wesleyan Methodist chapels were functioning. In addition other non-conformist bodies were operating throughout the county with 14 Congregational chapels, 11 Primitive Methodists, 8 Presbyterian, 3 Church of Scotland, 3 Independent, 4 Baptist and 4 United Methodist.

In Westmorland the earliest Wesleyan Methodist chapel opened in 1814 at Kendal and by 1850 there were 17 with 9 representing other denominations.

By that date non-conformity in Lancashire north of the sands, made no impact, perhaps because it was a Quaker stronghold.

[11] Nora Ratcliff (ed.), *The Journal of John Wesley* (Nelson, 1940).

A distribution map (see Map 21) of the Wesleyan Methodist Chapels shows that they were concentrated in West Cumberland and in the middle reaches of the Eden valley. The impact of industry had already been felt in the former area, but it is more difficult to justify the cluster in the latter area. It is away from the main north-south highway although the area is a fertile one and the parishes are numerous. So far as Furness was concerned industry did not really develop until after 1850 with the tremendous development of Barrow.

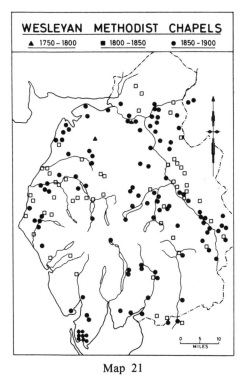

WESLEYAN METHODIST CHAPELS
▲ 1750 – 1800   ■ 1800 – 1850   ● 1850 – 1900

Map 21

The middle of the nineteenth century was in many ways a turning point in Cumbria. The region consisted of the Diocese of Carlisle and part of the Diocese of Chester north of Morecambe Bay with 155 parishes. But by then non-conformity had established itself mainly in the Carlisle Diocese rather than in that of Chester, with concentrations in the east and west and there were just over 120 chapels functioning.

Major developments were still mainly peripheral with the central mountainous area relatively unchanged in the religious sense from medieval times. Thus the major geographical influence of relief still held good, but new elements were coming to the fore, both economic and social. Geological formations were there to enable the region to take advantage of new technology and world markets to establish heavy industry related to coal and iron. This in its turn caused upheavals in society with greater urbanisation and the weakening of close community life enjoyed through the ages in rural villages. The Church was losing its influence as the chief welfare organisation as the State took on more responsibility for the welfare of its citizens. Up to then it had had a monopoly in the field of education but this too was beginning to go.

So for the hundred years 1850 to 1950 economic and social factors fashioned the organisation and observances of religion throughout Great Britain. Cumbria was no exception. First the Carlisle Diocese was enlarged, to be followed by a great increase in the number of parishes and an accompanying increase in non-conformist units.

CHAPTER 7

Some factors influencing the size and shape of parishes in Cumbria

During this account of the parishes of Cumbria questions may be asked about their size and shape, and a digression may be profitable to avoid repetition later. It is apparent that the fixing of parish boundaries was the result of evolutionary processes some of which were related to social and economic considerations, the distribution of population and of settlement and land use patterns as well as cultural and historical traditions. But most of these would tend to explain size, rather than shape and actual siting, although it is always dangerous to generalise. For instance one might expect that the parish would have its church as near to its geographical centre as possible, particularly in the early days when travel was not easy, yet attendance compulsory. But an account of Castle Sowerby belies this: "The church . . . is situate at the very extremity of the parish the reason of which probably might be as in many other instances, that the founder (who was most commonly the lord of the manor) did inhabit nigh thereunto. And to this day we see in abundance of parishes the church and manor house to be nearly contiguous".[1]

However certain deductions are justified and in an area like Cumbria with its great variety of topography it is easy to see the extent to which physical features influence both size and shape of parishes and in some cases the actual siting of the settlement round which the parish grew. In the *History of Antiquities*,[1] many instances are given to illustrate this point. Uldale for example "is long and narrow, being straitlaced by the mountains on the east and the Elne on the west and extending itself from south to north above four miles in length though it be not a mile in breadth anywhere". Or Caldbeck, "runs from west to east in length above seven miles from the Thornystone to the head of Mossdale, being hemmed in on the fourth side by a ridge of mountains called Caldfell,

---

[1] *History and Antiquities of the Counties of Westmorland and Cumberland*, chap. 7 (1777).

Caldbeck fells, Noonfell and Carrock". These two illustrations show the influence of the highest land, where boundaries tend to follow the watershed and also the lower land where rivers act as good dividers although rivers do sometimes change courses bringing administrative problems.

A cross section of part of Cumberland from approximately west to east showing parish boundaries will illustrate further (see Map 22).

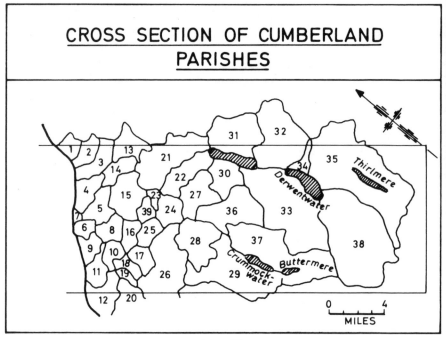

CROSS SECTION OF CUMBERLAND PARISHES

Map 22

From the coast in the west there is a broadish stretch of coastal plain stretching roughly from 5 to 10 miles before the land rises towards the central dome of the Lake District in the east in the Great Gable, Scafell and Helvellyn area, deeply scored by the Derwentwater and Bassenthwaite valleys, Thirlmere, Ennerdale and Wastwater; the traditional isolated regions. So far as the size of parish is concerned it is clear that relief has been at least one of the determinants. The smallest in area are all in the western lowland part, with size increasing with height in the eastern region. Compare for instance, Embleton, Cockermouth (2 parishes), Brigham and Broughton (Nos. 23, 24, 25 and 16 on the Map) with St. John's-in-the-Vale, Borrowdale, Thornthwaite and Buttermere (Nos. 35, 38, 33 and 37 on the Map). The only exception is No. 34 Keswick, the smallness of which is accounted for by the fact that it is the largest settlement and focal point of the highland areas. This generalisation could also be argued for in relation to the relative densities of population which is of course intimately connected with relief. Taking the higher land first two possibilities occur; (a) a valley is an economic unit and where it is deep seated and limited in extent parishes tend to be elongated following the contours allowing for enclosed land in the valley bottom and for open sheep runs on both upper slopes in order to make a viable economic unit. This is seen in the parishes of St. John's-in-the-Vale and Borrowdale, although it must be appreciated that these were not parishes in their own right in medieval times, but chapels of ease in the parish of Crosthwaite (Keswick). Grasmere, too, is a good example of this as Map 23 shows. Nor are

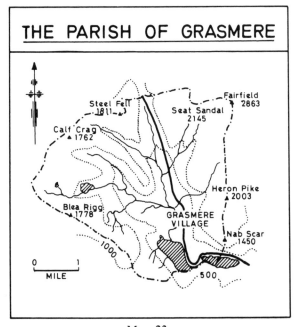

Map 23

such limitations restricted to parishes. In the upland areas the spheres of influence of non-conformist chapels were determined to a large extent by land configuration, as is illustrated by Map 24 showing the distribution of the subscribers in 1900 to the Methodist chapel at Outhgill in the long deep narrow valley of Mallerstang to the south of Kirkby Stephen. The other possibility is where a valley contains

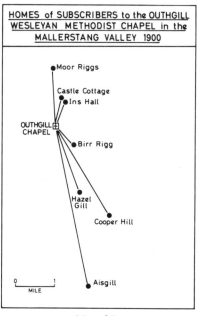

Map 24

sufficient cultivatable land in its lower parts along with open moorland grazing to make the river the parish boundary with two settlements one on either side. This is seen in Buttermere and Loweswater (Nos. 37 and 36 on Map 22), but this type of parish (where boundaries tend to run across the contours) is best seen further east in the Eden valley in parishes such as Dufton, Murton, Warcop and Musgrave (see Map 25). Here each parish has a share in the different types of land, from meadows in the valley bottom, through some arable land of the lower slopes to the open fell grazing land. Returning to the lowland area in the north-west of Cumbria two physical controls operate. Along the

Solway coast there is a considerable amount of very low land, marshy in places and sandy. In this less fertile area the size of parishes increases when compared with more fertile areas further south. Such parishes are, Bowness, Burgh-by-Sands, and the three Holmes (Holme Cultram, Holme St. Cuthbert and Holme St. Paul). On the other hand further

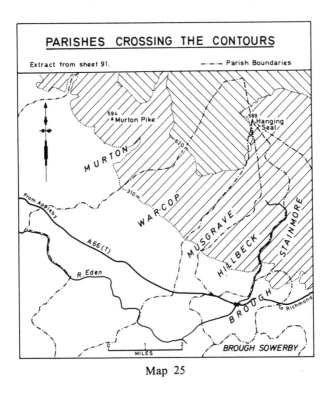

Map 25

inland is a region of glacial deposition with a number of drumlins. As the *History of Antiquities* of 1777 states of Aspatria – "It stands upon the ridge of a hill, pointing east and west in length above half a mile upon a dry sand".

Parishes in this area tend to be grouped round drumlins because they act as dry point sites in a region of less good drainage. Such parishes in addition to Aspatria are Hayton, Bromfield and West Newton (see Map 5).

So it is apparent that configuration of the land with its impact on human settlement and on communications, played a large part in determining the size and shape of parishes. This influence continued to be important up to the nineteenth century and the Industrial Revolution when other factors came into play, which will be discussed in the appropriate chapter.

CHAPTER 8
The Religious Census of 1851

At this point of time it is possible to take stock of the overall position of religious observance in Cumbria, as in the whole of England and Wales, for in 1851 there occurred the first – and last – religious census. It was a census of church attendance and was carried out on Sunday, March 30th on a national basis when the clergyman, minister and pastor of every place of worship was required to provide the following information:

(a) the denomination of each place of worship
(b) the number of sittings provided
(c) the total number of attendances – morning, afternoon and evening – on that day.

This is not the appropriate place to go into the shortcomings of the census and therefore the degree of validity of its findings; these are pointed out by John Gay[1] who gives an account of the census and the compilation of results. But no account was taken of double or triple attendances, nor the reliability or otherwise of the enumerating cleric and in fact some clergy did not bother to send in the returns. The actual findings were published in 1854 by Horace Mann who had been given the task of assembling the information.[2] One method of interpretation was devised by K. S. Inglis[3] who took the total attendance of the day of each unit and expressed it as a percentage of its total population, but without taking into account multiple attendances. This percentage he termed the Index of Attendance and thus some idea of the strength of each denomination could be ascertained. The table below sets out an

[1] J. D. Gay, *The Geography of Religion in England* (Duckworth, 1971).
[2] H. Mann, *Report on Religious Worship in England and Wales founded on the 1851 Census* (London, 1854).
[3] K. S. Inglis, *English Churches and the Working Classes 1880-1900* (Oxford, 1956).

Index for Cumbria, modified to take into account the number of non-returning churches. By this time the Methodists had split and each branch is shown separately.

1851 Religious Census

Denomination	Index of Attendance		Manns' original figures with estimates added based on % of churches not returning	
	England	Cumberland	Westmorland	North Lancashire
Church of England	30·2	less than 25	25 to 33	less than 25
Roman Catholic	2·2	1·1 to 2	0·1 to 1	nil
Methodist	14	less than 10	10 to 15	10 to 15
Baptist	4·5	less than 3	less than 3	less than 3
Presbyterian	0·5	1 to 2·9	0·3 to 0·9	0·3 to 0·9
Congregationalists (Independents)	5·9	less than 4	less than 4	4 to 6
Methodists				
Calvinistic	—	—	—	0·6 to 1
New Connexion	—	—	—	0·01 to 0·5
Original Connexion	—	5·1 to 10	5·1 to 10	5·1 to 10
Primitive	—	2·1 to 5	2·1 to 5	0·01 to 0·5
Bible Christians	—	—	—	0·01 to 0·5
W. Methodist Association	—	over 2·5	0·6 to 1·5	0·6 to 1·5
W. Methodist Reformers	—	—	0·01 to 0·5	0·01 to 0·5

Taken from John D. Gay

First in general terms the lowest attendances in England as a whole were in the large towns, as low as 25% in some cases, with absentees particularly among the urban working classes, the Index being 71·4% for rural areas and 49·7% for large towns. The total attendances registered were over 10 million, almost equally divided between the Church of England and the non-conformists. The figures published were:

Total attendances in England	10,896,066
Church of England	5,292,551
Roman Catholic Church	383,630
Others	5,219,885

This was assessed to mean that only about 50% of the population attended a place of worship on that day, a fact which came as a surprise and shock to those in high places. But it must be remembered that 30th March 1851 was a very wet day throughout Britain and many of the clergy making the returns mentioned the fact that attendances were below normal due to the inclement weather. The index figures show that in terms of total attendances Cumberland and North Lancashire were well below average for Church of England, Roman Catholics, and nonconformists, Cumberland sharing the lowest place along with the counties of Northumberland and Durham and Metropolitan London. This is somewhat surprising in view of the fact that Cumbria was still a rural area in general with the greatest urban expansion still to come. Of the non-conformists the Methodists were the largest body in Cumbria, particularly in Cumberland, although below the English average, and of course they were much divided. The original Methodist group – the Original Connexion – had most adherents, followed by the Wesleyan Methodist Association and the Primitive Methodists, the Association perhaps because of the traditional independence of Cumbria people and the fact that the Association came into being as a result of rebellion against the "dictatorial attitude" of the Methodist Conference. The presence of Presbyterians is interesting because they were strongest in the north of Cumberland round Cockermouth and Longtown, where Scottish influence on the border would be strongest. In the south only one congregation, at Kendal, is recorded. The Congregationalists were weak in Cumberland and Westmorland compared with other parts of the country, a fact which probably reflects the lack of funds in a traditionally poor area to maintain buildings and ministers since such chapels had to be self financed.

So on the whole it would seem that Cumbria's record of religious observance on that day in 1851 confirms the fact that allegiance to the Established Church was in decline with the weakening of ties which bound the closely knit rural communities. There was considerable social change and in the early part of the nineteenth century there had been many enclosures with the resultant commuting of tithes for land which caused antagonism among the farming community. It was not until 1834 that tithes in kind were abolished. Many parishes were held in plurality with an underpaid curate in charge whose quality left much to be desired. The resident rector was often a member of the aristocracy or the squirearchy, emphasising still more the gulf between the various social classes. In the towns the Church was not geared to the new situation of industrial expansion and failed to cater for the majority of people. Even the non-conformists were below strength in Cumbria although as will be seen in the next chapter they became much more successful in the second half of the century when their flexibility of organisation proved to be better able to cope in urban areas. The Established Church was hampered by the fact that it was based on a rigid parish system.

CHAPTER 9
1851-1950 – The Age of Steam and the Urban Explosion

So by 1850 the industrial revolution was well under way and the country was poised for the tremendous upheaval economically, technically and socially which occurred during the reign of Victoria. It was during the fifty years to 1900 that changes in religious observance and practice were at their greatest.

The great importance of communication has been stressed more than once already, but the invention of steam power with the resultant construction of the railways and the steamships of iron instead of wood, saw the greatest leap forward in the mobility of people and commodities. This matched the tremendous increase in productive capacity which the factory system brought. At the same time the countries of the world, epitomised in the creation of the British Empire, were ready to receive the industrial products which the British Isles were ready to make and the railways and shipping routes were ready to move those products both within our frontiers and beyond them.

The traditional routeways through Cumbria had been largely determined by the relief of the area making use of the lower land and particularly the river valleys wherever possible. So it is not surprising that since railway construction was closely related to gradient the new iron routes corresponded fairly closely to the existing road system even to the extent of a proposed barrage across Morecambe Bay to correspond with the route "across the sands". George Stephenson actually prepared plans for such a railway route but nothing came of it. Before this however in 1834 a steam packet started to ply between Liverpool and Ulverston, and by 1847 there was a service between Fleetwood and Barrow (Piel) which was by then linked with Dalton by the Furness railway. Meanwhile the railway had reached Lancaster and Fleetwood from the south in 1840 (hence the Fleetwood-Barrow packet) and by 1846 the Lancaster-Carlisle section was opened using the Lune and Eden valleys. From this line there were to be two branches; from Oxenholme to Kendal and Windermere (then called Applethwaite) opened in 1847, and from Carnforth to Barrow-in-

Furness opened in 1857. In the north, Carlisle was linked to Maryport in 1846 and later in 1848 this line was extended southwards via Workington and Whitehaven to Millom and Barrow thus linking the two areas of greatest industrial potential. Carlisle was linked to Newcastle-on-Tyne by 1840, and Silloth in 1856. The Workington-Cockermouth line was opened in 1847 and continued via Keswick to Penrith in 1863. Other routes reaching further into the heartland of the Lake District were Ulverston-Lakeside, 1869, Foxfield-Coniston 1859, Ravenglass-Boot (Eskdale) 1875, this last being only a narrow gauge line. The Coniston and Boot lines were essentially for the carrying of minerals, the former for copper ore which was exported via Piel, and the latter for iron ore. The Workington-Penrith line linked with one from Penrith to Northallerton via Stainmore with the specific purpose of facilitating the movement of coking coal from Durham to West Cumberland for smelting purposes and iron ore to Durham from West Cumberland for the iron industry there. The last construction was completed in 1875 between Settle and Carlisle via Appleby. Not surprisingly with the importance of West Cumberland increasing as an industrial area, a network of local lines linked the iron and coal locations, for example the Workington-Cleator Moor branch in 1879.

So Cumberland, Westmorland, and Lancashire 'north of the sands' lost some of their isolation and between 1850 and 1900 three major changes of a geographical nature took place which affected the total number and distribution of population. First and foremost was the development of industry in West Cumberland and Furness respectively, both as a result of the geology of the area and particularly in the case of the latter because of its coastal situation. Second came the increase in size of some, although not all, of the market towns such as Penrith, Ulverston, Wigton, Kendal, Cockermouth and of course Carlisle which once again regained its position as the leading town, the administrative and episcopal centre of the region. These market towns were the foci of routes, roads and rail, and thus the collecting and distributing centres as a result of which various industries developed as well. Thirdly, at last the heartland, the mountainous dome, was 'discovered' and opened up. The rugged beauty of the volcanic rocks mirrored in the various lakes brought tourists to Windermere, Ambleside, Grasmere and Keswick, with steamers on Lakes Windermere, Ullswater and Coniston.

The great increases in population created the need for more parochial units but it was not only parish boundaries that needed sub-dividing. In England generally the existing dioceses could no longer function satisfactorily, for not only was the population increasing in number, but its distribution pattern was changing. 'Cumbria' as has been seen was affected by these changes. With the advent of the railways, Carlisle became again the main centre of the north-west region, and with the industrialisation of South Lancashire the Chester Diocese could no longer cope with such a large area. Consequently in 1836 the church commissioners recommended "that the Sees of Carlisle and Sodor and Man be united and that the diocese consist of the present Diocese of Carlisle, of those parts of Cumberland and Westmorland which are now in the Diocese of Chester, of the Deanery of Furness and Cartmel in the county of Lancaster, of the parish of Aldeston now in the Diocese of Durham, and of the Isle of Man". With the exception of Aldeston and the Isle of Man an Order in Council of 1847 authorised the change, but since the holder of the See of Carlisle, Bishop Percy, withheld his consent the new and present diocese did not come into being until 1856 with the consecration on 13th April in that year of Henry Montagu Villiers as Bishop. So the new Diocese of Carlisle consisted of the counties of Cumberland (less Alston area), and Westmorland along with that part of Lancashire north of the Sands, i.e. Furness and Cartmel (see Map 1). In it there were 155 parishes; 109 from the old Carlisle Diocese and 46 from the new additions. Initially it was divided into the Deaneries of Carlisle, Allerdale, Westmorland, Cumberland, Coupland, Kendal, Furness, Cartmel and Lonsdale, but these divisions were soon to change although internal changes do not affect this account.

The growth of industry with the resultant increase in urban population was most marked in West Cumberland (Allerdale and Coupland) and in Furness where it was centred on Barrow-in-Furness. Here, perhaps better than anywhere else can be seen the impact of urban growth on both the Anglican and Non-conformist bodies and confirms what has already been said about these two main religious groupings in their attitude to changing social conditions.

In 1850 Barrow was still only a small settlement with a population of 660 and this mainly because of the four jetties from which iron ore was exported. Census-wise Barrow was part of Dalton, the traditional centre of the area and part of Dalton parish. The port was still under the jurisdiction of Lancaster Port although it acquired its first Commissioners in 1848. But census returns for the period 1850 to 1900 show how dramatic was the change:

1851 (with Dalton)	4,500 (Barrow 660)
1861 ,, ,,	9,000 (1864 Barrow – 8,176)
1871 (Barrow alone)	18,911
1881 ,, ,,	47,259
1891 ,, ,,	57,712
1901 ,, ,,	57,586

The accompanying time chart shows just what happened (see Fig. 1). By 1860 the railway network was almost complete, the first of the iron mines was in operation with further iron ore finds at Park, near Askam-in-Furness which proved to be the second greatest haematite deposit in Britain. The annual output of ore rose from 182,000 tons in 1849 to 336,829 tons in 1855, with 200,000 tons sent from Barrow to South Wales, Staffordshire, West Riding and Cleveland. This output exceeded that of West Cumberland by almost 100%. In 1859 the largest haematite deposits were found at Hodbarrow near Millom and from then on iron smelting, using coke from Durham brought by rail, became a major industry. The Hindpool furnaces were erected in 1859 to be followed by those at Hodbarrow in 1866 and at Askam in 1867. All this activity sparked off other industries and the expansion of the port. Steel making by the Bessemer process began in 1865 and by 1867 there were engine and carriage works, shipbuilding, hemp and wire rope making, cranes and dock fittings, bridge and girder construction, engineering and building. In 1863 the Barrow Harbour Bill was passed to be followed in 1867 by the opening of the Buccleuch and Cavendish Docks entered through a newly dredged channel. Thus the centre of population moved from Dalton to Barrow. What of religious activity to look after the spiritual needs of the new inhabitants? J. D. Marshall writes: "It can be said that during the first two decades of Barrow's growth the dissenters made most of the running and most truly represented the religious leanings of its people."[1]

The first Anglican church, St. George, was erected on Rabbit Hill in 1859-60 as a chapel of the parish of Dalton. It was largely the result of

[1] J. D. Marshall, *Furness and the Industrial Revolution* (Barrow-in-Furness, 1958).

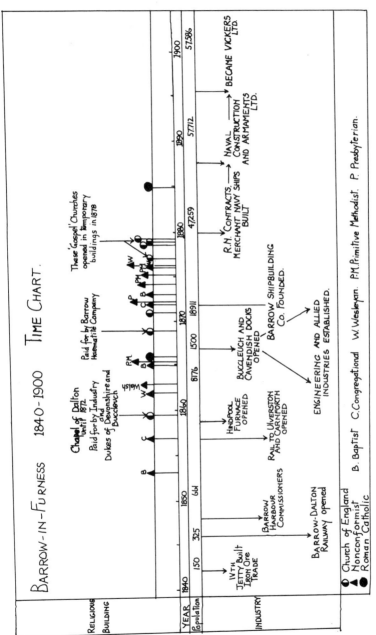

Fig. 1

efforts by Sir James Ramsden and paid for by various industries and the Dukes of Devonshire and Buccleuch, the two largest landowners in the area. It remained a chapel of ease in Dalton parish until 1872. The Church of St. James was opened in 1869 so that by 1870 there were two Church of England churches functioning. On the other hand by that date there were eight non-conformist chapels, the first a Baptist, in 1853 on Walney Island. There followed in 1857 an Independent chapel at Hindpool enlarged in 1863, in 1862 a Wesleyan chapel, in 1865 a further Baptist chapel and two Primitive Methodist buildings, while in 1863 a Welsh chapel was built to cater for the seamen from the ore boats. To serve the needs of an estimated 1,300 Roman Catholics, St. Mary of Furness opened in 1866.

The development of Barrow continued with the setting up of the Barrow Shipbuilding Co. in 1871 starting as the Haematite Iron and Steel Co. in 1859, extremely important for the town, for in its first decade it constructed Royal Navy contracts as well as merchant ships, and became the biggest employer of labour in the town and district before the end of the century as 'Vickers', and so it has remained. In the 1870s the Anglican church became more active with St. Pauls Newbarns in 1871, St. Luke 1877, St. Matthew 1879, St. John 1879 and St. Mark 1879. The dissenters were equally busy with a further seven chapels. So between 1850 and 1880 seven new parishes had been created out of Dalton parish and 15 non-conformist chapels built. There was a further Roman Catholic church in 1885.

In the surrounding area too, new parishes were created, again mainly out of Dalton parish; Ireleth with Askam 1874, Rampside, 1887, Dendron 1892, and Walney 1899.

The boundaries of the new parishes were not the result of an evolutionary process enclosing self-contained communities, but the result of the exigencies of technological and industrial development. They no longer served the needs of groups of people who saw themselves as a functioning unit and who appreciated their interdependence. The Anglican church was slow to appreciate this fundamental change, unlike the non-conformists who were never concerned with strictly defined boundaries. They (the non-conformists) were much more concerned with accessibility particularly in the rural areas so that the siting of a chapel took into account the road and rights of way pattern rather than a settlement nucleus. This is illustrated by

Map 26 showing the residential distribution of subscribers to the Methodist chapel at Gaisgill in 1900. Its siting and sphere of influence

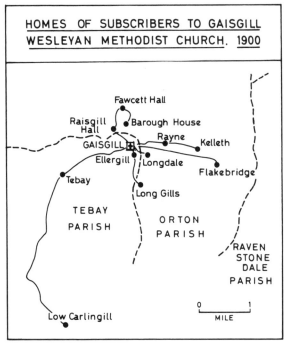

HOMES OF SUBSCRIBERS TO GAISGILL
WESLEYAN METHODIST CHURCH. 1900

Fawcett Hall

Raisgill
Hall
Barough House
Rayne
Kelleth
GAISGILL
Ellergill
Longdale
Flakebridge
Tebay
Long Gills
TEBAY
PARISH
ORTON
PARISH
RAVEN
STONE
DALE
PARISH
Low Carlingill

0   1
MILE

Map 26

was determined by the meeting of minor roads with the main Tebay-Kirkby Stephen road (now A685) on the boundary of the parishes of Tebay and Orton. Along with Map 27 of the domicile of members of the Asby United Methodist Free Church in 1900 it also illustrates the scattered nature of its supporters and the distances they were prepared to travel before the advent of the internal combustion engine.

The same sort of story could be told of West Cumberland with its coal and iron industries and the usual ancilliary concerns. Relevant population figures suggesting this are:

	1801	1851	1900
Arlecdon/Frizington	354	643	5,341
Cleator Moor	362	1,779	8,120
Egremont/Bigrigg	1,515	2,049	5,761
Workington	5,716	6,780	26,143

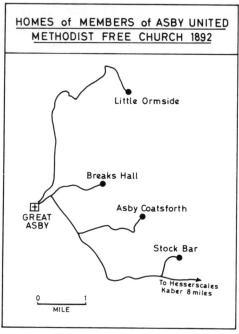

HOMES of MEMBERS of ASBY UNITED
METHODIST FREE CHURCH 1892

Little Ormside

Breaks Hall

GREAT
ASBY

Asby Coatsforth

Stock Bar

To Hesserscales
Kaber 8 miles

0   1
MILE

Map 27

The biggest expansion came in the second half of the nineteenth century and the new parishes correlate very well with this. They were Workington St. John 1835, Hayton 1868, Cleator Moor 1869, West Seaton 1893 and Maryport St. Mary 1893.

As has already been mentioned Non-conformity became relatively strong in this region with chapels being built in most reasonably sized settlements. For instance in Arlecdon there were two Wesleyan Methodist chapels built in 1829 and 1895 respectively, with a Primitive Methodist in 1875. In Frizington there were three chapels; Primitive Methodist 1876, Wesleyan Methodist 1884 and Christian Brethren 1892. It was in fact the Methodists who became the strongest non-conformist group, and they particularly who represented the flexibility in organisation which the rise in urban population needed. The parochial system was entrenched and change was slow and often came too late to allow the Established Church to maintain its former pre-eminence. J. D. Gay expresses the matter succinctly.[2] "Throughout the

[2] John D. Gay, *The Geography of Religion in England* (Duckworth, 1971).

expanding industrial north and the Black Country the Church of England's parochial machinery was unable to cater for the needs of the mushrooming population. Churches were too small, too few, badly endowed, badly staffed and unrealistically sited. Nobody could remember when changes had last been made. The inherited structures were hallowed by time and protected by legal safeguards. The essential quality of flexibility had been lost and so the Church of England was completely unable to adapt itself to the changed conditions. To insist on the population of a booming industrial town making a journey of several miles to its parish church was ludicrous in the extreme."

So much for the first of the geographical influences, the development of industry and the increase in urban population.

With the increase of population and the greater ease of transport with the coming of the railways, the market towns became more important as foci for geographical areas; as centres for services, as points of distribution and for administration. As they grew, they also attracted industries. In the north of the diocese Carlisle prospered. It had had a very chequered history as a 'border' town, but the coming of the railways gave it new life for once again it became the focus of routes; on the main west coast route London-Glasgow, and the east-west route from West Cumberland to Newcastle-on-Tyne, and Durham. Here came the Midland route from Leeds via Settle and Appleby continuing to Glasgow via Dumfries and Kilmarnock. It thus became the distribution centre for Cumberland as well as the county administration centre. Its population grew from 9,521 in 1801 to 26,310 in 1851 and 45,480 in 1901. In line with other towns it attracted industry, and became well known for biscuit making, metal industries and light engineering as well as textiles and industries associated with agriculture. It will be recalled that the two ancient parishes of Carlisle were St. Mary, formed from the Priory after the disssolution, and St. Cuthbert, with a third, Stanwix, north of the River Eden. No further changes took place until the nineteenth century when no fewer than seven new parishes were carved out. These were Holy Trinity 1834, Christchurch 1854, St. John, Upperby 1846, St. James, Denton Holme 1863, St. Stephen 1865, St. John 1867, St. Paul 1868. It will be noted that six of these came within a span of 15 years in the mid-century following on the main period of railway building and the establishment of industry. Three more parishes were to follow in the first half of the twentieth century, St. Aidan 1902, St. Barnabas 1934, and St. Herbert, Currock 1937. Non-conformity came early to Carlisle and by 1850 there were eleven chapels or churches; Church of Scotland 1, Presbyterian 1, Baptist 2, Congregational/Independent 2, Primitive Methodist 1, Wesleyan Methodist 2, United Methodist 1, Society of Friends 1. Before 1900 another eight had been added as well as fringe sects such as The Church of Jesus Christ of Latter Day Saints and the Salvation Army. Roman Catholics were represented by Our Lady and St. Joseph and St. Bede. The distribution is interesting for it shows the Scottish influence of the 'border' and the fragmentation of the Methodist persuasion which during the nineteenth century produced seven different worshipping groups. It is also interesting to note that prior to 1851 Methodism was least felt in Cumberland (as in Westmorland too), but after the mid-century it gained considerable support. The influx of Cornish miners into West Cumberland is given as one reason for this.

In the south of the diocese Kendal became the centre of administration and chief market town of Westmorland, although Appleby remained as the 'county' town. It had long been noted as a wool market and cloth-making town – 'Kendal Green' was famous – but with the coming of the canal from Preston and Lancaster in 1819 thus providing a link to the Lancashire coalfield, further expansion was encouraged. Near the canal terminus to the east of the River Kent, a carpet-making factory was built in 1822, to be followed by an iron works and an enlarged Castle Mills by 1855, which made railway rugs, coat linings and tweeds. Population increased to service these new industries which supplemented the traditional ones of cloth-making, marble polishing, papermaking and snuff manufacturing. Consequently during this period two new parishes came into being – St. Thomas (1832) and St. George (1841) carved out of Holy Trinity, the original parish church. But that is not the whole story. Kendal had been one of the largest parishes in Cumbria in early medieval days stretching as far as Grasmere and Langdale, and at one time having 39 curates. In 1777 it embraced 24 townships, a relic of the Danelaw manor and had 15 chapelries. This still obtained in 1850. (Windermere, Ambleside, Grasmere and Langdale were hived off much earlier.) In addition to Kendal there were Helsington, Natland, Scalthwaite, Rigg, New Hutton, Old Hutton with Holme Scales, Docker, Lambrigg, Grayrigg, Whinfell, Fawcett Forest, Whitwell and Selside, Skelsmergh and

Patton, Burneshead, Strickland Roger, Strickland Ketel, Long Sleddale, Kentmere, Crook, Winster, Over Staveley, Nether Staveley, Hugill, Underbarrow, Bradley Field. The 15 chapels were at Kendal, Helsington, Natland, New Hutton, Old Hutton, Grayrigg, Selside, Burneside, Long Sleddale, Kentmere, Crook, Winster, Staveley, Ings, Underbarrow. Obviously such a parish was quite unwieldy and with social and economic change which quickened in the second half of the nineteenth century and the first part of the twentieth along with increases in population, it was inevitable that new parishes were created. Moreover people were no longer prepared to travel miles to their church. Mention has already been made of the three parishes in Kendal. During this time the following further parishes received full parochial status: Mansergh 1866, Burneside 1929, Crook 1929, Staveley 1929, Underbarrow 1929, Ings and Hugill 1929, Skelsmergh with Selside and Long Sleddale 1913.

This fragmenting of the old medieval parishes occurred in many places in the Carlisle Diocese and practically all came during the period 1850-1930 (see Map 28). By 1900 there were 297 parishes of which 169 were in Cumberland. So much for the urban areas and market towns. Stress has already been made on the importance of railway construction, giving quick access to many parts of the Lake District from the developing conurbations to the south and east. Prior to this, the central dome area had been 'discovered' by writers and particularly poets, culminating in the 'Romantic' movement of the early nineteenth century. The background to this was geographical for it was the landscape of lakes and mountains, the rugged slopes of the more resistant volcanic rocks, the placid waters of the lakes, the wildness of Scafell and Helvellyn, the lushness of Windermere and Rydal which proved to be irresistible. One of the early visitors was Thomas Gray who wrote of Ullswater in his Lakes Journal in 1769, "From hence saw the lake directly at my feet, majestic in its calmness, clear and smooth as a blue mirror, with winding shores and low points of land covered with green enclosures, white farm houses looking out among the trees, and cattle feeding. The water is almost everywhere bordered with cultivated lands gently sloping upwards until they reach the foot of the mountains which rise very rude and awful with their broken tops upon either hand." But it was Wordsworth and his sister Dorothy who exerted most influence through their cult of 'nature'. They were

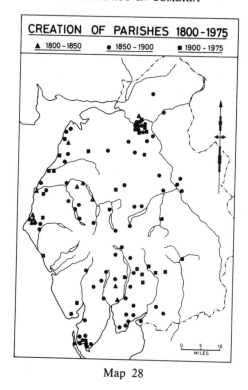

Map 28

essentially products of the 'dome' of the Lake District from their homes at Grasmere and Rydal and it was through them that others like Coleridge (Greta Hall, Keswick 1800-1804) and Southey (Greta Hall 1803-1843) came to live among the hills. Windermere, Grasmere, Ambleside and Keswick became fashionable focal points from which excursions could be made to most parts of the Lake District, and with the coming of railheads to Windermere, Keswick and Lakeside their popularity increased. Ruskin did the same for the Coniston area where he lived at Brantwood for 30 years beginning in 1871 and Coniston too became a railhead. Thus the relative isolation of the 'dome', the core of Cumbria was at last disappearing and this is reflected in the creation of new parishes in what up to then had been backward and static areas; Langdale 1863, St. Johns-in-the-Vale (Thirlmere) 1863, Matterdale 1865, Borrowdale 1865, Patterdale 1866, Wythburn 1867, Newlands

1868, Satterthwaite 1881, Troutbeck 1882, Lorton 1883, Buttermere 1884, Loweswater 1886, Windermere, St. John 1888, Coniston 1892. The construction of the Furness Railway from Carnforth to Barrow did away with the journey "across the sands" of Morecambe Bay, and made the Cartmel and Furness peninsulas much more accessible to the rest of the country and gave new life not only to Barrow, but also to the smaller settlements, the working villages such as Flookburgh and Allithwaite, and the resorts-to-be of Grange and Kents Bank. Consequently here too new parishes were created, Allithwaite 1866, Lindale 1872, Field Broughton 1875, Flookburgh 1879, Grange-over-Sands 1884, Witherslack 1891. Some of these had previously had chapels of ease and were townships of earlier manors.

So the second half of the nineteenth century saw the Church of England making efforts to respond to the new economic and social changes which brought about much redistribution of population. The greatest percentage increase in the number of parishes came in Furness and Cartmel, with West Cumberland (Allerdale) next. The accompanying graph shows just how important were the years 1850-1900 in the development of the Carlisle Diocese and in fact also illustrates the advances made in industry and agriculture in Cumbria.

During this period too, many churches were either rebuilt, newly built or structurally altered, for the Victorians were great 'restorers'. Between 1856 and 1869 restoration of a value of over £500 occurred in 53 churches while between 1869 and 1892 the number was 90. In all, during Bishop Goodwin's episcopate (1869-1891) 67 churches were built, rebuilt or restored in the Archdeaconry of Carlisle, 42 in Westmorland and 27 in Furness, a total of 136, nearly half of all the churches in the diocese. In fact very few escaped some alteration or refurbishment – unfortunate in many cases from the historical and aesthetic point of view. But churches were not in a fit state to deal with increased numbers and had been allowed to deteriorate in previous decades. Ulverston, a market and industrial town, is a case in point; the parish church of St. Mary by 1830 was proving to be quite inadequate for the number of worshippers. This, remember, was an age when most people felt an obligation to worship in a church or chapel. The population was about 3,000 in 1801 but by 1831 it had risen to 5,000. St. Mary's was still inadequate after being enlarged, so steps were taken to provide another building elsewhere in the town. The church of Holy

Trinity was consecrated in 1832 and eventually it became an independent parish in 1867 (see later for its decline and demise).

All this activity gives the impression that a strong and healthy Church existed and it is acknowledged that the disappointing figures produced by the Census of 1851 did not reflect the true position. Yet in view of the rapidly increasing population, particularly urban, the upsurge in building and refurbishment did no more than retain the status quo relatively speaking, thus indicating no real advance. During the second half of the nineteenth century the Scientific Revolution, led by such outstanding men as Charles Darwin and James Huxley affected the intellectuals. Many felt that the entire Christian cosmology was being undermined with the result that it was necessary to question the whole spectrum of Christian belief. In this way the Church's hold on many people was weakened.

When Bishop Villiers (1856-60) arrived in Carlisle he was not impressed with the state of his church or of that of his clergy, too many of whom were ill-equipped academically to meet the challenge of new ideas. He found that 11 livings were valued at less than £50 per annum, nine under £60, 16 under £70, 26 under £80, 21 under £90 and 35 under £100. So 118 clergy had an average income of only £83 per annum. Add to that the further effect of pluralism which in mid-century affected almost half of the benefices in the diocese, and the plight of many clergy can be appreciated. Bishop Waldegrave in 1862 reported that "there were still 47 villages without a church, 51 livings with no parsonage, and 96 benefices under £100 per annum and 64 under £150. Of the 33 University men ordained by Bishop Villiers, only 10 remained, of the 22 literates only three; the rest had gone south in search of better pay. Fifty parishes had no parochial collections, or if so only to meet some local want as the purchase of a harmonium."[3] There would seem to be a continued shortage of clergy, too many with low incomes and too many with a poor standard of education. This was not new; every bishop from 1133 onwards made similar complaints. Yet at the same time money was available for material improvements to buildings. Victorian philanthropy was not ashamed to display itself, often being an expression of success in industry or trade. Between 1860 and 1890 78 parsonages were built, rebuilt or improved.

[3] C. M. L. Bouch, *Prelates and People of the Lake Counties* (Kendal, 1948).

So during the second half of the nineteenth century, and to a less extent during the early years of the twentieth, one of the most important problems facing the various religious bodies was demographic; how to cope with an increasing population and one which was being redeployed so that not only were existing churches too small, but many were in the wrong places to meet the needs of urban dwellers. The parish system with its rigidly defined boundaries evolved centuries previously was geared to a stable rural society and could not cope with relatively quick changes in population distribution and was slow to react, so that, for instance, while between 1860 and 1875 in Barrow-in-Furness two Church of England buildings were built, the non-conformists had provided eight chapels. Of course the non-conformists were not bound by territorial boundaries and because of their greater flexibility as the need for a chapel grew so it could be provided when and where it became necessary, as opposed to the cumbersome process of creating a new parish. The dissenters, too, were more directly in touch with the new working class whose loyalities had to be created and could no longer be assumed.

The Methodists were the largest of the non-conformist groups and may be taken as examples of the dissenting half of the population. In Cumbria between 1850 and 1900 no fewer than 106 chapels were built, 63 in Cumberland, 36 in Westmorland and 7 in Lancashire north of the Sands. Many were in the rural areas where they were in direct opposition to the Established Church; they took advantage of the hostility aroused by the enclosures, which were often associated with the Church when tithes were commuted for land, and the squirearchy. The independence of spirit shown by the new industrial workers was beginning to be seen in the villages and it tended to be the chapel which provided self-respect for the labourer. It was the chapel which represented the new Liberalism. Map 21 shows the distribution of Methodist chapels. It will be noted that up to 1850 they corresponded pretty well with the earlier centres of population, concentrated in the Eden Valley and in West Cumberland. After 1850 there was much infilling in these areas, particularly in the lower Eden Valley, but with more in the south in line with industrial development and the opening up of communications round Barrow-in-Furness, and more also in the villages in the highland area of the dome such as Grange-in-Borrowdale, Grasmere, Mallerstang, and Patterdale. The era of

Methodist expansion was over by 1900. The other denominations, Baptists, Congregationalists, Presbyterians and Roman Catholics were not so strong as the Methodists. Although for them too the second half of the nineteenth century was a period of expansion. But by the early 1900s the major changes in population distribution had taken place and the location of the major industries had been established, so the drive for increased provision for religious observance waned. The period up to 1950 was one of great fluctuations between and during two World Wars when the whole attitude to Christian worship underwent great changes, with great repercussions for all denominations. Yet the number of parishes in the Carlisle Diocese continued to increase until the start of the Second World War in 1939 (see Graph 1). There were 23 new ones showing no particular pattern, being well spread out in both

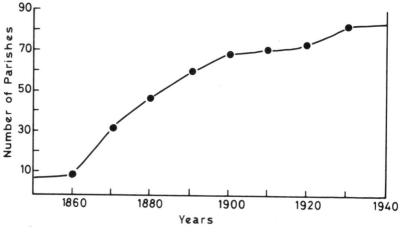

The Creation of New Parishes in the Carlisle Diocese 1850–1940

(Statistics taken from the Diocesan Registry)

Graph 1

urban and rural localities. For instance there were three in Carlisle (St. Aidan, St. Barnabus and St. Herbert) as befits the county town with a population rising to over 60,000 and single ones at Silloth and Maryport on the west coast, Waverton near Wigton on the Carlisle plain, Staveley and Burneside between Kendal and Windermere, Frizington in the West Cumberland industrial area and Seascale, a west coast resort. But the momentum had gone and other forces were beginning to operate which, after 1925, caused a reversal of policy to take place: the process of uniting benefices. Examples of this were Asby and Ormside (1927), Blawith and Lowick (1928), Cockermouth All Saints and Christchurch (1939), Castle Carrock and Cumrew (1941), Kirkbride and Newton Arlosh (1951) (also see Appendix).

The three maps (No. 29) of the parish boundaries in the Cartmel and Furness peninsulas admirably sum up the story of the evolution of parishes through the ages. From the time of their creation to the

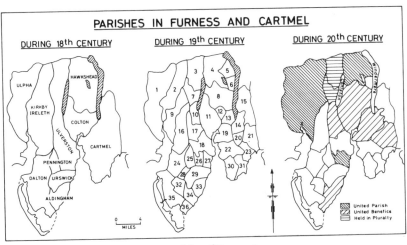

Map 29

eighteenth century there was relatively little change in their numbers. Then in the nineteenth century the effects of the industrial revolution brought about great changes in both population total and distribution with a consequent considerable increase in the number of separate parishes, while in the twentieth century with its great social upheavals and resultant materialism and scepticism, the number of separate parishes has declined.

The expansion of the Methodist Church was almost over by 1900 but it managed to maintain its position until the 1930s. Three Wesleyan Methodist Chapels were opened in Cumberland, Broughton Moor

(1903), Beaumont (1905), Hesket (1905), while in Westmorland there were four, Brough (1905), Dufton (1905), Milnthorpe (1904) and Stainmore (1909). In Lancashire north of the Sands there were at least eight at Barrow-in-Furness, Coniston, Dalton, Dendron, Egton-cum-Newland, Haverthwaite, Kirkby Ireleth, Pennington and Ulverston. The Methodist movement had been relatively weak in Cumbria prior to 1851 as the religious census showed, but it had become relatively strong by the early twentieth century. Yet even so, in 1932 the United, Primitive and Wesleyan Methodists united to form the Methodist Church, an action taken on economic grounds as well as religious, its effect in practical terms being an easing of the financial and manpower problems for it now became possible to close many chapel buildings. This differed from the policy of the Church of England which continued to support the same number of churches, the saving therefore being mainly on manpower.

The viewpoint of this study has been that up to the mid-twentieth century the story of Christian religious organisation and observance in Cumbria has had some geographical basis, with influences derived from the physical environment, from the structure and methods of agriculture, from technical advances in communications and industry resulting in movements of people, thus bringing about urban groupings as well as rural ones, and in some cases replacing them. In addition there has been a tremendous increase in the total population. Throughout of course too there has been the human element, the nature of the society through which religious activity exists. It would now seem that a change in emphasis was taking place with 'society' looming large and geography becoming of minimal significance. If this is so then the basis of our narrative changes.

CHAPTER 10
Trends 1950-1980

Since the Second World War of 1939-45, great changes have taken place in both the structure and attitudes of Society, with marked effect on religious organisation and worship. There is much greater emphasis on material than on spiritual well-being and the welfare of the individual is becoming more and more the prerogative of the State. The result in religious terms is that fewer people are attending places of worship, there is a decrease in the number of men presenting themselves for ordination to the priesthood or ministry, while inflation is causing financial problems for churches of all denominations collectively and individually.

It is extremely difficult to pinpoint the reasons for these present trends and it is more appropriate to look to the sociologists, philosophers, psychologists and politicians for the answers rather than to geographers. Nevertheless, there are certain consequences of a spatial nature which it is appropriate to deal with in this account.

The great increase in the number of separate parishes in the Established Church came to an end during the first half of the twentieth century and the reverse process is now happening in the second half (Graph 2). The rigid parochial divisions are having to disappear. By analysis of the numbers of Easter communicants and those presenting themselves for confirmation, it is found that dioceses in England with the highest density of population, i.e. those in industrial areas, have the lowest percentage of church members, while those with the lowest density, i.e. the rural areas, have the highest percentage. The Carlisle diocese with a large rural component belongs to the latter category with 139 per thousand total population being Easter communicants (surpassed only by Hereford, Gloucester and Worcester) and over 90 per ten thousand confirmation candidates compared to London's 40. These figures were for 1962.[1] Perhaps this reflects the fact that Cumbria is still a 'border' county where village life at any rate has been less

[1] J. D. Gay, *The Geography of Religion in England* (Duckworth, 1971).

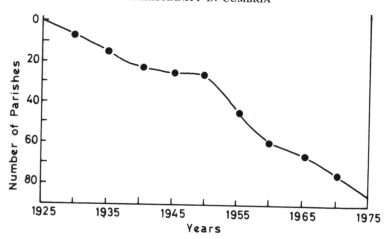

The number of Parishes in the Carlisle
Diocese Losing their separate Identities
1925 - 1975

(Statistics taken from the Diocesan Registry)

Graph 2

modified than elsewhere. Physical isolation still persists to some degree compared with other parts of the country. Yet while the Church in Cumbria may be stronger than in other parts of the country it has to face facts and bring about retrenchment through a modification in the parochial system. This is being done in four different ways; by creating (a) Pluralities, where two or more parishes retain their complete independence but share one priest; (b) United Benefices, where two or more parishes link together sharing one priest but each retaining its Parochial Church Council; (c) United Parishes where two or more parishes unite as one parish with one priest and one Parochial Church Council; (d) Team Ministries, where two or more parishes amalgamate with two or more priests sharing responsibility and each parish sending representatives to one Parochial Church Council. The Appendix (p. 135) details the position in 1980 when 110 parishes retained their complete single identity while 19 were held in pluralities. There were 54 United Benefices involving 144 parishes, 14 United Parishes involving 33 parishes and four Team Ministries involving 16 parishes. As was to be expected the greatest changes have come in the rural areas of less dense population spread over the whole area and not confined to the higher land of the centre. Even yet the Church of England generally has not completely adapted itself to the new situation. In 1970, three out of every four parishes were in rural areas while four out of five people lived in urban areas. It must be assumed therefore that so far as the Carlisle Diocese is concerned the most important single factor in these enforced changes is the shortage of clergy and therefore the necessity to deploy those available in the more urban areas. A comparison between the Rural Deanery of Appleby and that of Carlisle illustrates this point.

Similarly retrenchment has also taken place among the non-conformist groups. The amalgamation of the various branches of Methodism took place as early as 1932 when the one Methodist Church came into being. The result of this was that about 30% of Methodist chapels became redundant. "Without doubt there has been a very substantial re-aligning of Methodist churches and Sunday Schools. Furthermore, the auditorium type of church associated with many famous church names, has been replaced by a smaller building. Inevitably, the overall seating represented by these churches has been drastically reduced, and that trend has called for more flexibility in design and use of buildings."[2]

In 1972, the Congregational and Presbyterian groups joined together to form the United Reformed Church and the number of buildings in use decreased accordingly. Here again the shortage of ordained ministers has necessitated the linking of chapels, although not to the same extent as the Established Church since non-conformity has always made more use of the laity in conducting worship.

Thus the general trend is for Christian worship to be practised by less people both laity and ministry. But throughout the ages the Christian Church has faced many challenges and it has been the thesis of this book that in the north-west Celtic fringe of England its geography has played a significant part. Initially it was the physical landscape and its setting in the country which created difficulties of accessibility, yet produced tightly knit interdependent communities. Later it was changing economic conditions with the greater and more diverse use of the natural resources of the land, of crops and animals nurtured and

---

[2] The Methodist Church, Dept. of Chapel Affairs, *Statistical Returns*, pt. 1 (1972).

nourished by the monastic houses with the resultant strengthening of the religious life until their dissolution. But perhaps the greatest challenge of all came from the centuries of the agricultural and industrial revolutions when man's inventiveness produced new sources of energy and more sophisticated machines causing great upheavals in society and on redeployment of people, producing great urban sprawls. Such matters came within the scope of geography. But it is ultimately man who is the dynamic force and today it would appear that he has created a more complex society than ever before. Materialism and scepticism go hand in hand and greater affluence and security, both to be commended, seem to bring greater discontent which the things of the spirit fail to resolve. The way ahead is difficult to foresee, but history tells us that a way will be found and that others will be able to recount the continuing story of the Christian Church in Cumbria where this leaves off.

APPENDIX

Deanery and Parish Organisation 1980 – Carlisle Diocese

Taken from the Diocesan Registry 1980

Archdeaconry of Carlisle

Rural Deanery of Appleby

Single Parishes

Bolton, Crosby Ravensworth, Orton, Tebay.

United Benefices

Asby, Ormside;
Bampton, *Mardale;
Brough, Stainmore;
Kirkby Thore, Temple Sowerby, Newbiggin;
Long Marton, Dufton, Milburn;
Lowther, Askham;
Morland, Gt. Strickland, Thrimby;
Shap, *Swindale;
Warcop, Musgrave, Soulby, Crosby Garrett.

United Parishes

Appleby St. Lawrence, Murton-cum-Hilton;
Kirkby Stephen, Mallerstang;
Ravenstonedale, Newbiggin-on-Lune.

*No church

Rural Deanery of Brampton

Single Parishes

Arthuret, Brampton, Cumwhitton, Farlam, Hayton, Holme Eden, Scotby, Walton.

United Benefices

Blackford, Scaleby, Bewcastle, Stapleton;
Castle Carrock, Cumrew, Croglin;
Crosby-on-Eden, Irthington;
Gilsland, Nether Denton;
Kirklinton, Hethersgill, Scaleby;
Nichol Forest, Kirkandrews-on-Esk;
Rockcliffe, Blackford;
Wetheral, Warwick.

United Parishes
> Cotehill, Cumwhitton;
> Lanercost, Kirkambeck.

Rural Deanery of Carlisle

Single Parishes
> Bowness on Solway, Carlisle Holy Trinity, Carlisle Harraby, Carlisle Morton, Carlisle St. James. Carlisle Upperby, Carlisle St. John, Carlisle Stanwix, Dalston, Holm Cultram, Roughtonhead, Thursby, Wigton, Wreay.

Pluralities
> Aikton, Gt. Orton.

United Benefices
> Bromfield, Waverton;
> Burgh-by-Sands, Kirkbampton;
> Carlisle St. Aidan, Carlisle Christchurch;
> Carlisle St. Herbert, Carlisle St. Stephen;
> Kirkandrews-on-Eden with Beaumont, Grinsdale;
> Kirkbride, Newton Arlosh;
> Westward, Rosley, *Woodside, Welton.

United Parishes
> Caldbeck, Castle Sowerby, Sebergham;
> Carlisle St. Cuthbert, Carlisle St. Mary;
> Houghton, Kingmoor.

Team Ministry
> Carlisle Holy Trinity, Carlisle St. Barnabas.

*No church

Rural Deanery of Penrith

Single Parish
> Addingham with Gamblesby, Dacre, Gt. Salkeld, Kirkland, Lazonby, Martindale, Patterdale, Plumpton Wall, Watermillock.

United Benefices
> Barton, Pooley Bridge;
> Clifton and Brougham, Cliburn;
> Edenhall, Langwathby, Culgaith;
> Hesket-in-the-Forest, Armathwaite;
> Kirkoswald, Renwick, Ainstable;
> Penrith St. Andrews, Penrith Christchurch, Newton Reigny;
> Skelton, Hutton-in-the-Forest, Ivegill;
> Skirwith, Ousby, Melmerby.

Team Ministry
> Greystoke, Matterdale, Mungrisdale.

Archdeaconry of West Cumberland

Rural Deanery of Calder

Single Parishes
Arlecdon, Beckermet St. John, Egremont, Frizington, Gosforth, Haile, Hensingham, Kells, Mirehouse, Moresby, St. Bees.

United Benefices
Beckermet St. Bridget, Ponsonby;
Bootle, Cornby, Whicham, Whitbeck;
Cleator Moor, Cleator St. Leonard;
Seascale, Drigg;
Lamplugh, Ennerdale;
Eskdale, Irton;
Muncaster, Waberthwaite;
Wasdale Head, Nether Wasdale;
Whitehaven Holy Trinity; Whitehaven Christchurch.

United Parishes
Whitehaven St. James, Whitehaven St.Nicholas.

Rural Deanery of Derwent

Single Parishes
Borrowdale, Bridekirk, Brigham, Crosthwaite, Dean, Keswick St. John, Lorton, Mosser, Threlkeld.

United Benefices
Bassenthwaite, Isel, Setmurthy;
Bolton, Ireby;
Uldale, Loweswater, Buttermere;
Thornthwaite, Braithwaite with Newlands;
St. John-in-the-Vale, Wythburn.

Team Ministry
Cockermouth All Saints, Cockermouth Christchurch, Embleton Wythop.

Rural Deanery of Solway

Single Parishes
Broughton Moor, Camerton, Clifton, Cross Canonby, Dearham, Distington, Flimby, Great Broughton, Harrington, Holm Cultram, Maryport, Netherton, West Seaton, Workington St. John, Workington St. Mary, Workington St. Michael.

Pluralities
Allhallows, Torpenhow.

United Benefices
Allonby, Westnewton;
Aspatria, Hayton, Plumbland, Gilcrux.

United Parishes
Silloth Christchurch, Causewayhead.

Archdeaconry of Westmorland and Furness

Rural Deanery of Furness

Single Parishes
Barrow-in-Furness St. Aidan, Barrow-in-Furness St. James, Barrow-in-Furness St. John, Barrow-in-Furness St. Mark, Barrow-in-Furness Walney, Barrow-in-Furness St. Matthew, Barrow-in-Furness St. Paul, Dalton-in-Furness, Egton cum Newland, Ireleth with Askham, Kirkby Ireleth, Millom St. George.

Pluralities
Bardsea, Urswick;
Coniston, Torver.

United Benefices
Aldingham, Dendron, Rampside.
Barrow-in-Furness St. Luke, Barrow-in-Furness St. George;
Blawith, Lowick;
Millom Holy Trinity, Thwaites;
Pennington, Lindal, *Marton.

United Parishes
Broughton, Duddon, Dunnerdale, Seathwaite, Ulpha, Woodland;
Ulverston, St. Mary, *Ulverston Holy Trinity.

*No church

Rural Deanery of Kendal

Single Parishes
Arnside, Beetham, Burneside, Burton-in-Kendal, Crosscrake, Heversham, Holme, Augill or Ings, Kendal Holy Trinity, Kendal St. George, Milnthorpe, Natland, Preston Patrick.

Pluralities
Winster, Cartmel Fell, Crosthwaite, Witherslack;
Crook, Kendal St. Thomas;
Grayrigg, Old and New Hutton;
Levens, Underbarrow and Helsington.

United Benefices
Skelsmergh, Selside, Long Sleddale;
Staveley, Kentmere.

Team Ministry
Kirkby Lonsdale, Hutton Roof, Lupton, Casterton, Barbon, Middleton, Mansergh.

Rural Deanery of Windermere

Single Parishes

Allithwaite, Cartmel, Flookburgh, Grange-over-Sands, Grasmere, Langdale, Rydal, Sawrey, Troutbeck, Windermere St. John, Windermere St. Martin, Windermere St. Mary.

United Benefices

Colton, Satterthwaite, Rusland;
Haverthwaite, Finsthwaite, Staveley-in-Cartmel;
Lindale, Field Broughton.

United Parishes

Ambleside, Brathay;
Hawkshead, Low Wray.

BIBLIOGRAPHY

Annals of Kendal (Cornelius Nicholson, 1861).

BARNES, F., *Barrow and District* (Barrow, 1968).

BEDE, *Ecclesiastical History*, Everyman translation.

BOUCH, C. M. L., *Prelates and People of the Lake Counties* (Titus Wilson, Kendal, 1948).

BOUCH, C. M. L. & JONES, G. P., *The Lake Counties 1500-1830 – A Social and Economic History* (Manchester, 1961).

BOWEN, E. G., *Saints, Seaways and Settlement* (University of Wales Press, 1969).

BOWEN, E. G., *Settlements of the Celtic Saints in Wales* (Cardiff, 1956).

BOWEN, E. G., 'Britain and the British Seas 1902-1962', *Geography at Aberystwyth* (Dept. of Geography, Cardiff, 1970).

Cambridge Medieval History, 'The Victory of the Papacy', vol. 6.

Carlisle Diocesan Directory, 1980.

CHADWICK, H. K. & OTHERS, *Studies in the Early British Church* (Cambridge University, 1958).

COLLINGWOOD, W. G., *The Lake Counties* (J. M. Dent, 1902), (1947 edition).

COLLINGWOOD, W. G., *Lake District History* (Kendal, 1925).

CUMBERLAND AND WESTMORLAND ANTIQUARIAN AND ARCHAEOLOGICAL SOCIETY, *Transactions*, n.s., vols. viii, x, xi, xxi, xxiv, xxv, xlvi, xlvii, lvi, lvii, lix.

ECKWALL, E., *Concise Oxford Dictionary of English Place-Names* (1951), (3rd edition).

FERGUSON, R. S., 'A History of Cumberland', *County History Reprints* (S. R. Publishers, 1970).

FRASER, G. M., *The Steel Bonnets (Border Reivers)* (1971, Barrie and Jenkins Paperback – Pan Books, 1974).

FREEMAN, E. A., 'The Place of Carlisle in English History', *Archaeological Jl.*, vol. 39.

GAY, JOHN D., *The Geography of Religion in England* (Duckworth, 1971).

History and Antiquities of the Counties of Westmorland and Cumberland (1777).

History of the County of Cumberland, vol. 1, 'Pre-Norman Remains'; vol. 2, 'Ecclesiastical History' (Victoria County Histories).

INGLIS, K. S., *English Churches and the Working Classes 1880-1900* (Oxford, 1956).

JACKSON, K. H., *Studies in the Early British Church*, 'The Sources for the Life of St. Kentigern' (Cambridge University, 1958).

Kelly's Directory of Cumberland and Westmorland (1894).

MANN, H., *Report on Religious Worship in England and Wales Founded on the 1851 Census* (London, 1854).

MARSHALL, J. D., *Furness and the Industrial Revolution* (Barrow, 1958).

METHODIST CHURCH, THE, DEPT. FOR CHAPEL AFFAIRS, *Statistical Returns*, pt. 1 (1972).

MILLWARD, R. & ROBINSON, A. *The Lake District* (Eyre & Spottiswoode, 1970).

MOORMAN, J. R. H., *A History of the Church of England* (Adam & Charles Black, 1961), (2nd edition).

NICHOLSON, F. & AXON, E., *The Older Non-conformity in Kendal* (Titus Wilson, Kendal, 1915).

NICHOLSON, N., *Cumberland and Westmorland* (Robert Hale, London, 1949).

Place-Names of Cumberland, The, English Place-Names Society (Cambridge).

RAISTRICK, A., *Quakers in Science and Industry* (David & Charles, 1968).

RATCLIFF, NORA (ed.), *The Journal of John Wesley* (Nelson, 1940).

ROLLINSON, W., *A History of Man in the Lake District* (Dent, 1967).

SHAW, R. C., *Post-Roman Carlisle and the Kingdoms of the North-West* (Preston, 1964).

SMITH, W., *An Economic Geography of Great Britain* (Methuen, 1949).

THOMAS, CHARLES, *The Early Christian Archaeology of North Britain* (Oxford University, 1971).

THOMSON, P. D., *Parish and Parish Church* (Nelson, 1948).

TREVELYAN, G. M., *English Social History* (Longmans Green, 1948 ed.).

United Methodist Free Churches Register of Members (1891-99).

Valour Ecclesiasticus – Tempore Henrioii VIII Institutus, vol. 5 (1825).

Wesley, Rev. John, The Works of, vols. I to IV (London, 1829).

Wesleyan Methodist 20th Century Fund, Kirkby Stephen and Appleby Circuit (1900).

WEST, T., *The Antiquities of Furness, Ulverston 1813* (London, 1774).

Index